Lab Projects to accompany

MEDIA GRAPHIC PRODUCTION

Second Custom Edition

weekly Read ch 8, 9, 10

Taken from:

Adobe®After Effects® 6.5 Magic
by James Rankin and Anna Ullrich
with Jason Croatto and Danielle Hietmuller

3ds max® 4 Magic
by Sean Bonney
with contributions from Laurent M. Abecassis, Sue Blackman, Peter Draper, Richard Katz, Randy M. Kreitzman, Daniel Manahan, Michael Reiser, and Marcus Richardson

Updates to second edition by Eric Regner

Custom Publishing

New York   Boston   San Francisco
London   Toronto   Sydney   Tokyo   Singapore   Madrid
Mexico City   Munich   Paris   Cape Town   Hong Kong   Montreal

Cover image: courtesy of PhotoDisc/Getty Images.

Taken from:

Adobe® After Effects® 6.5 Magic
by James Rankin and Anna Ullrich
with Jason Croatto and Danielle Hietmuller
Copyright © 2005 by James Rankin and Anna Ullrich
Published by Peachpit Press
A Pearson Education Company
Berkeley, California 94710

3ds max® 4 Magic
by Sean Bonney
with contributions from Laurent M. Abecassis, Sue Blackman, Peter Draper, Richard Katz,
Randy M. Kreitzman, Daniel Manahan, Michael Reiser, and Marcus Richardson
Copyright © 2001 by New Riders Publishing
A Pearson Education Company
Indianapolis, Indiana 46290

This special edition published in cooperation with Pearson Custom Publishing.

Printed in the United States of America

10 11 12 13   V0CR   13 12 11 10

2008120082

KW

**Pearson
Custom Publishing**
is a division of

www.pearsonhighered.com

ISBN 10: 0-558-02739-3
ISBN 13: 978-0-558-02739-1

Many thanks to Paul Ashlin of the Rancho Cordova, California campus, ITT Technical Institute for his editorial review and selection of this textbook.

Contents at a Glance

Contents

Contents

CHAPTER 1 | Spinning Squares

In your work, you may often be asked to create something from nothing: no footage, perhaps just a logo and a few stills. In this chapter and the next, we'll show how much you can do with so little by working with the multitalented and jack-of-all trades (in the right hands, of course) Solid layer in After Effects.

Starting with only a company logo, you can pick a color palette and graphic style that work within the client's persona. For this project, you have three product shots and the company logo to work with. By focusing on four main colors (orange, green, purple, and yellow), you can build an engaging sequence for each product shot by using different shades and tints of each particular color to distinguish each segment.

It Works Like This

Check out the **Ch1_Finished_Movie.mov** file in this chapter's folder on the book's CD to see the 15-second advertisement you'll create in this project. The project uses solids to create interesting layouts from scratch and creates modular sequences that you can duplicate and easily modify to quickly build a cohesive presentation. You can take these skills and use them to create your own layouts out of solids or replace the solids with textures and other footage. The basic principles of this project are as follows:

1. Design interesting animations and layouts using nothing but solids.

2. Use solids to matte images of various sizes.

3. Use effects to transition from one sequence to another and to bring text onto the screen.

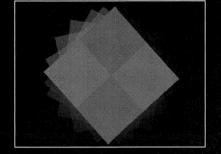

The spinning squares intro

Frame from the purple segment

The block dissolve transition

Preparing to Work

To prepare for this project, do the following:

1   Start with a new project, and import the **Images** folder from this chapter's folder on the CD. It contains the files **RainbowLamp.jpg, Sofa_01.jpg,** and **Rug.jpg.**

2   Create another folder named Graphics. Import Style_Logo.psd by using the Composition - Cropped Layers option (rather than Footage or Composition).

Import As Options: Do You Really Understand Them?

• *Footage*—You probably noticed long ago that when you import a layered file as footage, the file appears in After Effects either as if the layers have been flattened into one or with only a single layer that you pick. The layers are still there in the original source file, but you won't have access to the layers in After Effects. That's all well and good for some projects.

• *Composition*—When you choose this option for a layered file, the file is presented as a composition that contains an After Effects layer for each Photoshop layer. The composition has an associated folder in the Project window, which contains a footage item for each particular layer (handy!). In addition, any Photoshop layer that uses a Photoshop layer style is presented as a nested composition with a layer for each essential property in the layer style's effect. For example, a Photoshop layer that uses the Bevel and Emboss layer style will produce three layers in After Effects: a layer for the Photoshop layer, a layer for the style's shadow property, and a layer for the style's highlight property. This chapter's project takes advantage of this feature by animating a layer style contained in the logo.

• *Composition - Cropped Layers*—When you choose this option for a layered file, you get the same results you would for the Composition option, except for one crucial difference. The Composition - Cropped Layers option defines the dimensions of each layer according to the actual content within the Photoshop layer; in contrast, the Composition option defines the dimensions of each layer according to the dimensions of the entire file. This may sound like the Composition option stretches any layers that have smaller dimensions than the entire file, but it doesn't.

Building the Intro

You'll start this project by building the first modular component. Once it's built, you can duplicate it and modify it to quickly create the second part of the spinning intro, lickety-split.

Spin and scale, part 1

You'll begin by creating a snappy intro out of nothing but some orange, square-shaped solids:

1   Create a new composition named Horizontal Zoom, and set its dimensions to 720 × 540, the Frame Rate to 29.97, and the Duration to 5;00 seconds.

2   Create a new solid (Layer > New > Solid) named and colored Dark Orange (RGB: 236, 82, 2), with the dimensions 720 × 720.

3   Press the S key to display the layer's Scale property, and then set it to 25, 25%.

4   Duplicate the Dark Orange layer.

5   Select both layers in the Timeline, press A to display their Anchor Point properties, and then set the property for each layer as follows:

    Layer 1: 715, 715

    Layer 2: 0, 0

You've just set the landing position for the squares. Now you'll animate them onto the screen:

1   Go to time 0;20, select both layers, and press P to display their Position properties.

2   Add Position keyframes for both layers with the value 360, 270.

3   Go back to time 0;05, and move the top layer off the screen to the right (Position: 920, 270).

4   Move the bottom layer off the screen to the left (Position: –210, 270).

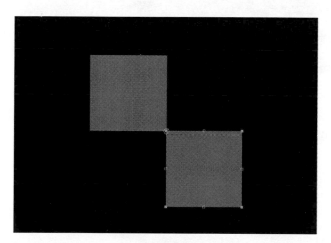

Both squares with new anchor points

Press the Home key and then the Spacebar to preview the animation. The squares should be offscreen to begin with and then slide in horizontally, pass each other, and stop kitty-corner to one another.

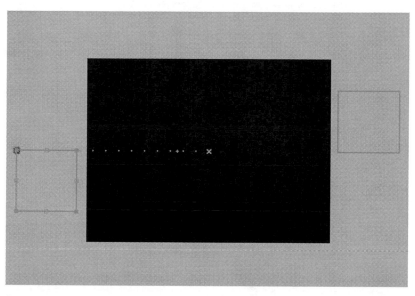

Composition with both squares offscreen on the gray pasteboard

To add a little more zip, let's make the squares spin after they pass each other:

1   Return to time 0;20, select both layers, and press the R key to display the Rotation property.

2   Add Rotation keyframes for both layers with the values 0 x +0.0.

3   Go to time 1;20, and change both layers' Rotation to –2 x +0.0. Now the squares rotate around the anchor point twice in a counterclockwise direction.

4   Press Shift+S to display the layers' Scale properties alongside Rotation. Click the stopwatch to add a Scale keyframe for both layers at time 1;20. (The Scale values should already be 25, 25% for both layers.)

5   Go to time 2;15, and change both layers' Scale to 50, 50%.

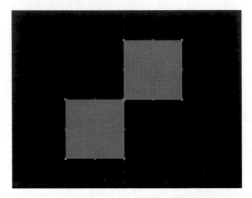

Timeline with Scale and Rotation keyframes revealed

Save and preview your work. The squares should slide in horizontally, pass each other, spin counterclockwise, and then scale outward. This is just half of the intro sequence.

Spin and scale, part 2

Next you'll modify a duplicate of the comp you just created in order to quickly create a vertical version of it:

1   Duplicate the Horizontal Zoom composition in the Project window, rename the duplicate Vertical Zoom, and then open it.

2   Rename and recolor both solids Mid Orange (RGB: 255, 107, 15).

3   Change each layer's Anchor Point property as follows:

Layer 1: 715, 0

Layer 2: 0, 715

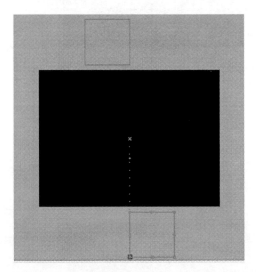

Squares in the Vertical Zoom comp with new anchor points

4   For each layer, move the Position keyframe at time 0;20 to time 0;15, and move the keyframe at time 0;05 to time 0;00.

5   Press Home to go to 0;00, and then change Layer 1's Position to 360, −200 and Layer 2's Position to 360, 740.

Both squares offscreen and on the gray pasteboard

That's it! The Rotation and Scale keyframes you need are already set up. Now the squares slide in from the top and bottom of the composition, pass each other, spin counterclockwise, and then scale outward.

Spin together

You're almost done with the opening animation. All that's left is to nest these two compositions in a third "parent" composition. First, you should organize the Project window:

1 Create a new folder called **Zooms,** and move the Horizontal Zoom and Vertical Zoom comps into it.

2 Select both Zoom compositions in the Project window, and drag them to the window's New Composition button. In the New Composition From Selection dialog, make sure Single Composition is selected, and click OK.

3 Rename the new comp *Intro* in the Project window.

Save and then preview your work. The squares should slide in from all four sides of the comp, form a square, spin counterclockwise, and then fill the comp window.

Building the Color Sequences

This project is created through a series of modular components. As you saw in the previous sections, you save lots of time by duplicating and altering sequences to create new sequences that create a cohesive whole. This process also lets you substitute different colors and content easily, without having to redo the entire project.

Orange sequence and a transition

Since you used orange squares in the intro, you'll use orange shades in the following sequence to create a smooth transition. If you want a more dramatic change, you can choose to use a different color for either section. Here are the steps:

1 Create a new composition named Orange Body, with dimensions of 720 × 540, Frame Rate 29.97, and Duration of 5;00 seconds.

2 Create a new solid named BG Orange, make it pale orange (RGB: 255, 194, 137), and make it comp size (click Make Comp Size in the Solid Footage Settings dialog).

3 Create a new solid named and colored Mid Orange (RGB: 255, 107, 15), and make it comp size too.

4 Set the Mid Orange layer's Scale to 60, 60%.

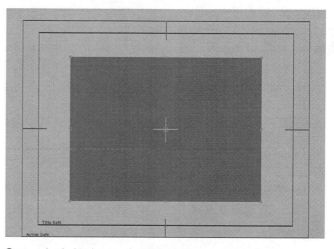

Orange body background and mid orange rectangle

The Transition effects in After Effects are generally used between scenes or to get an object on or off the screen. In this case, you'll use the Block Dissolve Transition effect to bring in an object:

1 Go to time 0;15, and apply Effect > Transition > Block Dissolve to the Mid Orange solid layer.

2 Set the effect's Block Width and Block Height properties to 20.0.

3   Set the Transition Completion property to 100%, and then click its stopwatch to create a keyframe for the property.

The settings for the Block Dissolve effect

4   Go to time 1;00, and change Transition Completion to 0%. Press Home and then the Spacebar to preview the transition.

Tip: Six of the seven Transition effects have a vital property named Transition Completion, which works like this: When the property is set to 100%, the layer is totally out of the scene; when the property is set to 0%, the layer is totally in the scene. Animate this property, and you've got yourself an instant slick transition.

---

5   Create a new solid named Pic Matte with dimensions of 432 × 324, using any color.

A matte is an easy way to set up a consistent size and position for any picture. No matter what picture you need to put in that spot, only the image area that lies within the matte's boundaries will display.

6   Position the Pic Matte layer at 360, 228.

7   Change its Scale to 100, 75%.

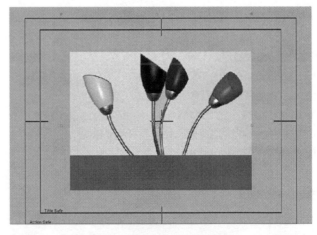

Positioning the blue photo matte

8   Add **RainbowLamp.jpg** to the Orange Body Timeline at time 1;00, and drag it under the Pic Matte layer.

9   Set the RainbowLamp layer's Track Matte to Alpha Matte "Pic Matte". Now the photo is matted by the Pic Matte layer.

Adding a Track Matte to the picture

10 Set the RainbowLamp layer's Position to 350, 280 and its Scale to 84, 84%.

The Pic Matte and photo in the Timeline

11 Still at time 1;00, add a 0% Opacity keyframe to **RainbowLamp.jpg.**

12 Go to time 1;10, and change the Opacity to 100%.

You're almost there. The position of the image is now set. Now you'll add a little text to the spot and apply a different Transition effect to bring it on:

1 Create a new text layer at time 1;10 that displays the text *That little something….* Use a really dark orange color (RGB: 214, 75, 3) and a font and text size that display the line of text within the orange rectangle beneath the image. (We used 40 for the Text Size, centered the text, and positioned it at 220, 410.)

2 Apply Effect > Transition > Linear Wipe to the text layer, and set the effect's Wipe Angle to 0 x +270.

3 Still at time 1;10, add a keyframe for 100% Transition Completion.

4 Go to time 1;20, and change Transition Completion to 0%.

Settings for the Linear Wipe effect

The sequence is nearly complete. Now you'll animate this section's opacity to create a transition to the next sequence:

1 Go to time 2;15, and select the text, matte, and photo layers.

2 Press T to display the layers' Opacity property, and then create a 100% Opacity keyframe for each layer.

3 Go to time 2;25, and change all three layers' Opacity to 0%.

Adding the fade out

4 Go to time 2;23, select layer 4 (Mid Orange), and create a Scale keyframe at the current size, which should be 60%, 60%.

5 Go to 3;08, and change the layer's Scale to 100, 100%.

Creating the screen wipe by animating Scale

Save and preview your work. The Orange Body comp should scale and wipe the screen.

Green sequence

When we chose the palette for the Style Design Center spot, we decided to work with a different color for each product section and the closing spot featuring the client logo. Since you're working with modular components, you'll be able to easily modify the Orange Body comp to produce a green version for the next sequence:

1   Duplicate the Orange Body comp, rename it Green Body, and then open it.

2   Rename and recolor the Pale Orange layer to Pale Green (RGB: 185, 217, 161) and the Mid Orange layer to Mid Green (RGB: 67, 179, 63).

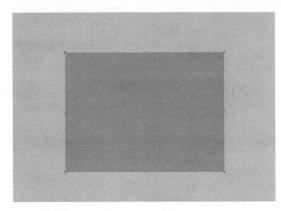

Changing the colors to make the green section

3   Select the RainbowLamp layer. Hold down Alt (Windows) or Option (Mac OS), and drag **Sofa_01.jpg** from the Project window onto **RainbowLamp.jpg** in the Timeline. This replaces the RainbowLamp image with the sofa image but retains the RainbowLamp layer's keyframes.

4   Scale the Sofa_01 layer to 68, 68%, and position it at 372, 300.

5   Change the Pic Matte layer's Position to 360, 310.

6   Change the text layer to display ...*extra special*..., change the text's color to a really dark green (RGB: 38, 106, 37), and position the layer at 255, 163.

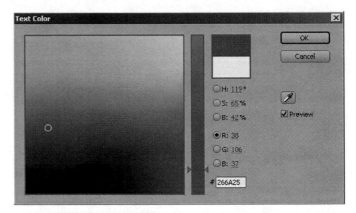

Changing the text's color

Save and preview your work. In just a few easy steps, you've designed the green sequence. You'll do the purple sequence using even fewer steps.

Purple sequence

Purple makes a nice third color choice because it's the complementary color to yellow, so the color transition between this section and the yellow-colored end tag really pops. Here are the steps:

1 Duplicate the Orange Body comp, and rename it Purple Body.

2 Rename and recolor the Pale Orange layer to Pale Purple (RGB: 187, 168, 255) and the Mid Orange layer to Mid Purple (RGB: 133, 79, 255).

3 Select the RainbowLamp layer. Hold down Alt (Windows) or Option (Mac OS) while dragging **Rug.jpg** from the Project window to replace the **RainbowLamp.jpg** layer in the Timeline and retain the layer's keyframes.

Leave the Position and Scale as they are.

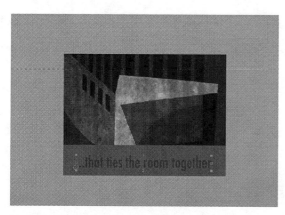

New colors for the purple section

4 Change the text layer to display ...*that ties the room together,* change the text's color to a really dark purple (RGB: 85, 50, 168), and position the layer at 177, 410.

Changing the text for the purple section

Save and preview your work.

Creating the End Tag

The section that will close your project will be kept pretty simple to keep the focus on the client's brand, but simple can still be fun (i.e., animated!).

Animating the effects

The client has given you their company logo: a beveled script text on top of a flat sans serif font. You'll make the logo come alive by animating the type's bevel, which is courtesy of a layer style that was applied to the logo beforehand in Photoshop:

1 Create a new composition named End Tag with dimensions of 720 × 540, Frame Rate 29.97, and Duration 5;00 seconds.

2   Open the "STYLE_LOGO" comp from the **Graphics** folder in the Project window.

The timeline for the Photoshop layer style

3   Go to time 0;10 in the "STYLE_LOGO" comp, and select both the Bevel Highlight and the Bevel Shadow layers.

4   Apply Effect > Transition > Radial Wipe to both layers.

5   Add a 100% Transition Completion keyframe to each layer.

Settings for the Radial Wipe effect

6   Go to time 0;20, and change each layer's Transition Completion property to 0%.

The logo is now a lot more interesting. Let's add it to the End Tag comp:

1   Return to the End Tag comp. Create a new solid that's named and colored Pale Yellow (RGB: 252, 253, 162) and that's at comp size.

2   Go to time 0;10, and drag the Style_Logo comp to the Timeline.

3   Add a 0% Opacity keyframe to the StyleLogo layer.

4   Go to time 0;20, and change the layer's Opacity to 100%.

Adding the fade in to the End Tag sequence

Save your work.

Completing the Finished Spot

You finally have all the pieces required to complete the final spot. You just need to assemble them and add some dissolves to soften the transitions:

1   Create a new comp named Final_Squares1 that's 720 x 540 in size, with Frame Rate 29.97 and Duration 15;00 seconds.

In order to have really smooth transitions, you need to add a cross fade between sections by animating the Opacity of each.

2   Add the Intro to the Final_Squares1 Timeline at time 0;00.

3   Go to time 3;00, and add the Orange Body comp to the Timeline.

4   Insert a 0% Opacity keyframe for the Orange Body layer.

5   Go to time 3;15, and change the layer's Opacity to 100%.

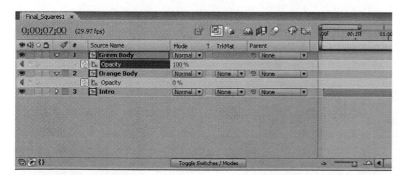

Timeline for the final comp with the Intro and the orange section

The green section comes next:

1   Go to time 6;15, add the Green Body comp to the Timeline, and add a 0% Opacity keyframe to the layer.

2   Add a 100% Opacity keyframe to the Orange Body layer.

3   Go to time 6;25, and change the Orange Body layer's Opacity to 0%.

4   Go to time 7;00, and change the Green Body layer's Opacity to 100%.

Adding the green section to the final comp

Now you add the purple section:

1   Go to time 10;00, add the Purple Body comp to the Timeline, and add a 0% Opacity keyframe to the layer.

2   Add a 100% Opacity keyframe to the Green Body layer.

3   Go to time 10;10, and change the Green Body layer's Opacity to 0%.

4   Go to time 10;15, and change the Purple Body layer's Opacity to 100%.

Adding the purple section to the final comp

The cross fade you'll create between the Purple Body comp and the End Tag comp is a little different than those you've created so far. The Purple Body takes exactly as long to fade out as the End Tag takes to fades in:

1   Go to time 13;15, add the End Tag comp to the Timeline, and add a 0% Opacity keyframe to the layer.

2   Add a 100% Opacity keyframe to the Purple Body layer.

3 Go to time 13;25, and change the Purple Body layer's Opacity to 0%.

4 Change the End Tag layer's Opacity to 100%.

Adding the yellow End Tag section to the final comp

Save and preview your work.

Tip: If you wish to cut down on render time, close the Timeline before rendering so After Effects doesn't have to display what it's rendering.

Now Try This

Congratulations! By now you've learned how easy it is to create a visually engaging spot from scratch using the extremely versatile Solid layer:

- Since After Effects treats solids like any other footage in the Project window, you can easily replace a solid with footage. Try replacing the Mid colored background layers with a moving texture or some footage.

- The mattes you've created allow you to put different items over the backdrop. Experiment by replacing the still image with video, or by adding an animated logo over the moving texture.

CHAPTER 2 | Falling Squares

After Effects provides some great prebuilt effects for creating scene transitions, but there's only so much you can do with them (or anything prebuilt!) when you want to make something unique. This chapter shows you how to design a lively transition that's simply made of animated solids. The transition features solids radiating outward toward the viewer and then collapsing inward to reveal a layout that's falling into place.

In the previous chapter, you worked almost exclusively with 2D solids to create cool and interesting effects. You'll use those same techniques in this chapter but add a bit of 3D and some dynamic animations to the brew. And since this project relies on solids for its transitions and layout, you can easily transform the solids even further or swap out the solids for your own content to make the project your own.

It Works Like This

Open the **Ch2_Finished_Movie.mov** file from this chapter's folder on the CD to see the spot you'll create. This project continues Chapter 1's theme of working with solids in place of video, animation, or other footage. In addition, you'll add some depth to the design by animating the solids in 3D space. The basic principles you'll use are as follows:

1. Use solids to create an enticing backdrop.

2. Matte images of various sizes using solids.

3. Create eye-catching transitions by animating solids.

4. Use Vector Paint to animate a Photoshop file's native effects.

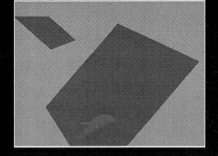
Solids rotating through space

The transition of radiating squares

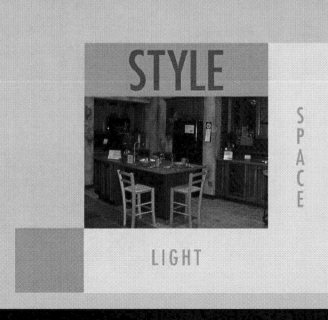
The green section of the product spotlight.

Preparing to Work

To prepare for this project, do the following:

1   Start with a new project, and create three folders named **Elements, Graphics,** and **Sections.**

2   Import the **Images** folder from this chapter's folder in the book's CD. This folder contains the following files:

  - **Chair_02.jpg**
  - **Chandelier.jpg**
  - **Kitchen_02.jpg**
  - **Bedroom_01.jpg**
  - **Television.jpg**

3   Using the Import As option Composition - Cropped Layers, import the **Style_Logo.psd** file from the CD into the Graphics folder.

Building the Transitions

The transitions you'll build in this chapter are inspired by retro designs of the 1960s and 70s. There's a positive madness for all things retro these days, which just so happens to work well with solids that are left in their "natural" state.

The orange transition

The idea behind the transitions is simple: a set of concentric squares that radiates out to wipe the screen and then comes back in to reveal a new scene. Simple, yes, but really snazzy, too!

You start with the squares:

1   Generate a new comp named Orange Squares in the **Elements** folder, with dimensions 720 × 540, Frame Rate 29.97, and Duration 4;00.

2   Create a new solid at 0;00 named Mid Orange (RGB: 255, 107, 15) with dimensions 720 × 720.

3   Create a 0% Scale keyframe.

4   Go to time 0;10, and change the Scale to 100%.

5   Duplicate the layer twice. Change the color of layer 1 to light orange (RGB: 255, 139, 52) and the color of layer 2 to dark orange (RGB: 236, 82, 2), and then rename both layers according to their new color.

Adding the scale change and duplicating the layers

Right now the three squares scale simultaneously, but you only see the top light-orange layer. So, you'll stagger the In points of the layers to make the squares appear to radiate outward:

1   Select layer 2, and go to time 0;03.

2   Press [to bring the layer's In point to time 0;03.

3   Select layer 1, and go to time 0;06. Press [to bring the layer's In point to time 0;06.

4   Select all the layers, and copy them.

5   Go to time 0;09, and paste the new layers.

6   Press Shift while dragging the layers, and snap the first frame of the Mid Orange layer to the Current Time Indicator (CTI).

Duplicating the layers so there are six squares

Scaling squares

You should now have squares that radiate out from the center of the screen with a three-frame offset between each layer. Very cool. Of course, there's more to do! Now you'll make the squares collapse back inward:

1   Go to time 1;05, and insert a 100, 100% Scale keyframe for layer 1.

2   Go to time 1;15, and change the Scale to 0%.

3   Copy these two keyframes.

4   Go to time 1;08, and paste the keyframes on layer 2. Paste the keyframes again on the remaining layers at the following points in time:

> Layer 3: 1;11
>
> Layer 4: 1;14
>
> Layer 5: 1;17
>
> Layer 6: 1;20

The staggered Scale keyframes

The squares should now radiate out for 25 frames, hold for 10 frames, and then collapse into the center for 25 more frames.

Save your work, and preview the animation.

Generating the other transitions

You need to create the same transition in the other three colors chosen for this spot:

1   Duplicate the Orange Squares comp three times, and rename the copies Green Squares, Purple Squares, and Yellow Squares.

2   Open the Green Squares comp. Rename and recolor the orange squares to the corresponding green hue: Light Green (RGB: 79, 217, 74), Dark Green (RGB: 45, 126, 43), and Mid Green (RGB: 67, 179, 63).

Changing the colors to shades of green

3   Repeat this process for the Purple Squares and Yellow Squares comps: Light Purple (RGB: 154, 127, 255), Dark Purple (RGB: 99, 58, 190), and Mid Purple (RGB: 133, 79, 255); and Light Yellow (RGB: 250, 253, 85), Dark Yellow (RGB: 187, 165, 57), and Mid Yellow (RGB: 199, 201, 67).

Save your work.

Building Backdrops

Now you have the transitions you need for the final. These bold graphics should reveal an impressive layout underneath. It's time to start exploring the 3D aspect of the project. Next you'll create the background elements for each section using nothing but our multi-talented friend the solid.

Fun with 3D

If you're getting tired of the flat solid, this is the part you've been waiting for. You'll give your solids a little more punch and depth by spinning them in three-dimensional space until they land in place in your layout:

1   Create a new composition named Moving BG Orange with dimensions 720 × 540, Frame Rate 29.97, and Duration 10;00.

2   Create a new solid named BG Square 1 with dimensions 720 × 720 in a mid orange color (RGB: 255, 107, 15).

3   Duplicate the layer.

4   Go to time 3;00, and insert a composition marker (Shift+1.) This marker lets you quickly return to this point in time by pressing the 1 key.

5   Turn on the 3D switch for each layer in the Timelines's Switches column.

6   Set the Position of BG Square 1 to 360, 270, 88, and add a Position keyframe.

7   Set BG Square 1's Scale to 48, 48%, and add a Scale keyframe.

8   Set the Position of BG Square 2 to 596, 32, 88, and add a Position keyframe.

9   Set BG Square 2's Scale to 18, 18%, and add a Scale keyframe.

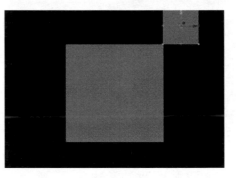

Creating the 3D squares background

You've positioned the squares where you want them to land after they spin in space. Working backward, now you need to make them spin into place:

1   Go to time 0;00, and create the following keyframes for the BG Square 1 layer:

    Position: 360, 270, 0 (animating the solid's position on the Z - axis from 0 to 88 makes the solid appear to move away from the viewer)

Scale: 110, 110, 110

Orientation: 0, 0, 0

X Rotation: 0 x +0.0

2 Still at time 0;00, create the following keyframes for the BG Square 2 layer:

Position: 592, 38, 0

Scale: 50, 50, 50

Orientation: 0, 0, 0

Y Rotation: 0 x +0.0

3 Press 1 on the keyboard to return to time 3;00.

4 Add the following keyframes for the BG Square 1 layer:

Orientation: 0, 0, 270

X Rotation: 2 x +180

5 Add the following keyframes for the BG Square 2 layer:

Orientation: 0, 0, 270

Y Rotation: 1 x +180

Adding the Rotation and Position keyframes

Save your work, and then preview the animation. The orange solids fill the entire Comp window and then rotate away from the viewer and stop spinning.

Creating the backdrop in multiple colors

Naturally, you need this fabulous backdrop in different colors for each sequence. Duplicate the Moving BG Orange comp twice. Rename the new comps Moving BG Green and Moving BG Purple. You could leave the squares where they are and change only their colors. However, the finished spot will be more eye-catching if you alter each background slightly.

Green

For the green sequence, leave the large solid where it is, and make the small solid land at the lower-left corner of the large solid instead of at the upper right:

1 Open the Moving BG Green comp, and change the color of both solids to a mid green (RGB: 67, 179, 63).

2 At time 0;00, change BG Square 2's Position to 80, 530, 0.

3 Press 1 to go to time 3;00, and then change the Position of BG Square 2 to 121.3, 508.7, 88.

New layout for the green background

Purple

For the purple sequence, make the small solid land at the upper-left corner of the large solid:

1 Open the Moving BG Purple comp.

2 Change the color of both solids to a mid purple (RGB: 133, 79, 255).

3   At time 0;00, change BG Square 2's Position to 70, 4, 0.

4   Press 1 to go to time 3;00, and then change the Position of BG Square
    2 to 123.3, 33.5, 88.

New layout for the purple background

Save your work.

Building the Sections

Are you ready to start engineering the final masterpiece? All the elements
you'll use to build the main body sections of the final are now complete;
you just need to put them together. You'll create a polished stage on which
your client's ever-important product information will shine.

The orange section

First you'll create a mellow background and position your backdrop:

1   Create a new composition named Section1_Orange in the **Sections**
    folder, with dimensions 720 × 540, Frame Rate 29.97, and Duration
    10;00.

2   Add the Orange Squares comp at time 0;00.

3   Go to time 0;28, and create a new solid named BG Orange that's
    comp size and pale orange (RGB: 255, 194, 137).

4   Drag the solid layer under the Orange Squares comp in the Timeline.

5   Go to time 1;00. Drag the Moving BG Orange comp to the Timeline,
    and position it so it's layer 2.

6   Change its Position to 346, 325.

Beginning to build the orange section

The spot will look more professional and work much better if the transitions interact with the elements they're revealing. The setup doesn't have
to be elaborate—you'll simply tweak the transition's position so the transition interacts with the backdrop:

1   Go to time 1;29, and add a Position keyframe of 560, 100 to the
    Orange Squares layer. Doing so lines up the final radiating orange
    square with the small orange solid's resting position.

Adding the Position keyframes to the transition

2 Return to time 0;00, and change the Position of the Orange Squares layer to 78, 476. Now the orange squares radiate outward starting from the lower-left corner of the composition.

3 Go to time 0;25. You should tweak the Orange Squares layer's position so that it covers the entire comp during the transition to the Moving BG Orange comp. Add a Position keyframe of 360, 270, and then copy the keyframe.

4 To hold the Orange Squares layer in that position during the transition, go to time 1;06 and paste the keyframe you copied.

5 Scrub the frames between the two keyframes you just created. You'll notice that the Orange Squares composition moves around even though the two keyframes have the same coordinates. To fix this, select the keyframe at time 0;25, and choose Animation > Toggle Hold Keyframe.

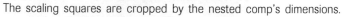

Timeline with the Hold keyframe

Play back what you have so far, and note how the Orange Squares comp crops the squares as they scale outward. To fix this, turn on the Collapse Transformations switch for the Orange Squares comp layer. Now the layers aren't confined by the dimensions of the Orange Squares composition.

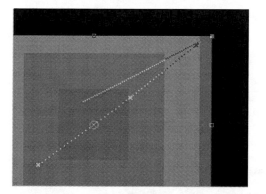

The scaling squares are cropped by the nested comp's dimensions.

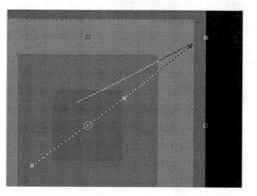

The Collapse Transformations switch reveals the layers entirely.

Matting a photo

Next, let's begin adding the client's product photos:

1 Go to time 4;00, and add a composition marker (Shift+2).

2 Create a new solid called Pic Matte that has dimensions of 720 × 720 and is any color. (Since you'll be using this solid as a track matte to frame and crop the product photos, the color doesn't matter as long as it's different from the mid orange color so you can see it in the Comp window as you work.)

3 Set the Scale (44.1, 31.5) and Position (346, 278) of the Pic Matte so it takes up the top two thirds of the larger orange square.

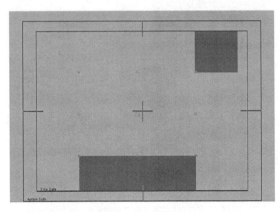

Adding the Pic Matte

4 Add the **Bedroom_01.jpg** file to the Timeline, under the Pic Matte layer. Notice that the image fills the entire composition.

5 Change the Bedroom_01 layer's Track Matte to Alpha Matte "Pic Matte". The image is cropped to the Pic Matte layer's dimensions.

6 Change the Position of the Bedroom_01 layer to 360, 260 and the Scale to 65, 65%.

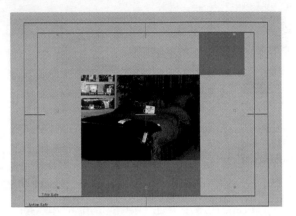

Adding the Track Matte to the picture

7 Add a 0% Opacity keyframe.

8 Go to time 4;10, and change the Opacity to 100%. Now the product image fades in after the orange squares land in place.

Adding text

The images are all in place, but they're only half of your visual symphony. Let's bring in another movement: text. You'll start with an element that will remain consistent throughout the project:

1 Press 2 on the keyboard to return to time 4;00.

2 Create a new horizontal text layer that displays the word STYLE in a dark orange color (RGB: 214, 75, 3). (For the other text properties, we used Futura Condensed Medium, size 92 pixels, and centered.)

3 Move forward in the Timeline so you can see the photo. Move the text so it's centered in the mid orange area under the photo. (We used Position 344, 475.)

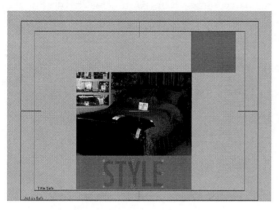

Creating the STYLE text element

Next, you'll create a horizontal graphic element to serve as a backdrop for text you'll place above the photo:

1 Press 2 to return to time 4;00.

2 Create a new solid layer named Horizontal Bar that has dimensions 720 × 110 and is colored a pale orange (RGB: 255, 232, 206).

3 Position the Horizontal Bar at 436, 110 so its bottom edge lies along the top edge of the big square.

4 In the Timeline, drag the Horizontal Bar layer so it's just above the BG Orange layer.

5 Apply the Linear Wipe effect (Effect > Transition > Linear Wipe) to the Horizontal Bar layer.

6 Set the effect's Wipe Angle to 0 x +270.

7 Add a Transition Completion keyframe of 100%.

8 Go to time 4;10, and change the Transition Completion property to 30%. Now the solid slides in from left to right.

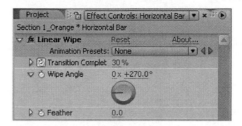

Settings for the Linear Wipe effect

Now you'll create a vertical version of the backdrop you just created, for the left side of the photo:

1 Copy the Horizontal Bar, and then paste it at time 4;02.

2 Rename the duplicate solid to Vertical Bar, and change its dimensions to 110 × 540 and its color to RGB 255, 232, 206.

3 Position the Vertical Bar at 129, 326 so its right edge lies along the left edge of the big square.

4 Change the Vertical Bar's current Wipe Angle keyframe to 0 x +0.0.

5 Go to the Vertical Bar's next keyframe at time 4;12, and change the Transition Completion to 21%.

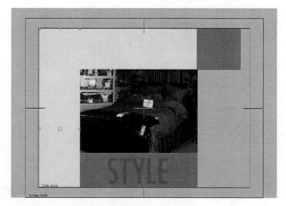

Adding the color bars

Now that you have your backdrops, you can add the last two text elements. The first is a vertical element that scrolls on the screen and then fades to a lighter color:

1   Create a new horizontal text layer that displays *STYLE* in a dark orange color (RGB: 214, 75, 3). (For the other text properties, we used Futura Condensed Medium, size 92 pixels, and centered.)

2   At time 4;13, add a vertical text layer that displays *PERSONAL* in a dark orange color (RGB: 214, 75, 3). (For the other text properties, we used Futura Condensed Medium, size 36 pixels.)

3   Position the text so the top of the P is about even with the top of the picture (about 133, 310).

4   Apply a Linear Wipe effect (Effect > Transition > Linear Wipe).

5   Set the Wipe Angle to 0 x +0.0.

6   Create a 100% Transition Completion keyframe.

7   Go forward 15 frames by pressing Ctrl+G (Windows) or Command+G (Mac OS) and entering +15 in the dialog.

8   Change the Transition Completion to 0%.

9   Go to time 5;08, and add a 100% Opacity keyframe.

10 Go forward 15 frames, and change the Opacity to 50%.

Fading down on the text

The final text element is horizontal and lies above the photo. It also scrolls on and fades out:

1   Go to time 5;08, and create a horizontal text layer that displays *EXPRESSION* in a dark orange color (RGB: 214, 75, 3). (For the other text properties, we used Futura Condensed Medium, size 36 pixels.)

2   Position the layer at 330, 127.

3   Apply a Linear Wipe effect (Effect > Transition > Linear Wipe) to the layer.

4   Set the Wipe angle to 0 x +270.

5   Create a 100% Transition Completion keyframe.

6   Go forward 15 frames, and change the Transition Completion to 0%.

7   Go to time 6;03, and add an Opacity keyframe at 100%.

8   Move forward 15 frames to time 6;18, and change the Opacity to 50%.

Adding the second text layer

The orange section is now complete. Save and preview your work.

Creating the green section

Once again, you'll use the duplicate-and-modify technique to create the other sections. You've probably already guessed that, since the 3D moving squares background is laid out differently, it will require you to make some adjustments to placement. Let's forge ahead into green territory:

1   Duplicate the Section1_Orange comp, and rename the duplicate Section2_Green. Open the Section2_Green comp.

2   Delete the Moving BG Orange layer, and replace it with the Moving BG Green composition.

3   Select the Orange Squares layer, and then hold down Alt (Windows) or Option (Mac OS) while dragging the Green Squares comp onto the Orange Squares layer.

4   At time 0;00, change the Position keyframe of the Green Squares layer to 560, 110.

5   At time 1;29, change the Position to 132, 426.

    The keyframes at time 0;25 and time 1;06 remain at 360, 270 to effectively wipe the screen.

6   Rename the BG Orange layer to BG Green, and change its color to a pale green (RGB: 185, 217, 161). (Leave the remaining settings alone.)

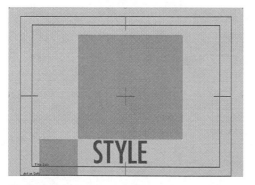

Changing the small square's position for the green layout

In order to add more visual interest, you'll move the picture matte relative to the background:

1   Press 2 to go to time 4;00.

2   Reposition the Pic Matte layer to 375, 289, and then duplicate it.

3   Select the Bedroom_01 layer, and hold down Alt (Windows) or Option (Mac OS) while dragging the **Chandelier.jpg** image to replace the Bedroom_01 image in the Timeline. The Chandelier image inherits the keyframes and position in time.

4   Scale **Chandelier.jpg** to 55, 55%, and Position it at 372, 295.

5   Go to time 5;13, and add a 100% Opacity keyframe to the layer.

6   Go forward 15 frames, and change the Opacity to 0%.

Adding a cross dissolve

To get more bang for the buck out of this section, add a second picture that will cross-fade with the other image:

1   Go to time 5;13, and add **Kitchen_02.jpg** to the Timeline.

2   Drag the layer under the topmost Pic Matte layer.

3   Set Kitchen_02's Track Matte to Alpha Matte "Pic Matte".

4   Set its Scale to 41, 41% and its Position to 376, 270.

5   Add a 0% Opacity keyframe to Kitchen_02.

6   Go forward 15 frames, and change the Opacity to 100%.

Section 2_Green ×

0;00;05;28   (29.97 fps)

	#	Layer Name	Mode	T	TrkMat	Parent		
	1	T EXPRESSION	Normal		None	⊙ None	
	2	T PERSONAL	Normal		None	⊙ None	
	3	T STYLE	Normal		None	⊙ None	
	4	☐ [Pic Matte]	Normal		None	⊙ None	
	5	● [Kitchen_02.jpg]	Normal		Alpha	⊙ None	
		Opacity	100%				
	6	☐ Pic Matte	Normal		None	⊙ None	
	7	● Chandelier.jpg	Normal		Alpha	⊙ None	
	8	Green Squares	Normal		None	⊙ None	
	9	Moving BG Green	Normal		None	⊙ None	
	10	☐ Vertical Bar	Normal		None	⊙ None	

Toggle Switches / Modes

Adding a second image to the composition

If you preview the composition from time 4;00 to 6;00, the chandelier photo should fade out while the kitchen image fades in at the same location.

Next, you need to move the vertical and horizontal bars to match the rest of this layout:

1   Go to time 4;00.

2   Select the Vertical Bar layer, and press the [key to bring the layer's In point to the current time.

3   Change the color of the Vertical Bar and Horizontal Bar solids to RGB 215, 254, 188.

4   Move the Vertical Bar to Position 589, 353, and move the Horizontal Bar to 572, 458.

5   Press U to reveal all keyframes for the Horizontal Bar layer, and then change the layer's final Transition Completion keyframe to 40%.

Moving the color bars to fit with the green layout

Of course, you need to change the text elements. You'll also change the timing of the linear wipe so it looks better with the length of the shorter words:

1   Select the STYLE text layer, and change the color to a really dark green (RGB: 38, 106, 37).

2   Change the layer's Position to 375, 165, so the text is centered in the green space above the picture.

3   Go to time 4;13, select the EXPRESSION text layer, and press [to move the layer's In point to the current time.

4   Change the text to say *LIGHT,* and change the color to a really dark green (RGB: 38, 106, 37).

5   Position the text at 375.5, 465.5 so it's centered under the picture.

6   Press U to reveal the text layer's keyframes.

7   Go to time 5;03, and select the final Transition Completion keyframe and both Opacity keyframes.

8   Drag the selected keyframes, and press Shift to snap the Transition Completion keyframe to the CTI. Doing so increases the duration of the linear wipe to 20 frames to account for the shorter word (and shifts the opacity fade-out).

Changing the text

9   Change the PERSONAL text layer to say *SPACE,* and change its color to darkest green (RGB: 38, 106, 37).

10   Position the layer at 589, 288 so it lies to the left of the photo.

11   Go to time 5;18. With the SPACE layer still selected, press [to move the layer's In point to the current time.

12   Go to time 6;18, and press U to reveal the layer's keyframes.

13   Select the last three keys, and drag to the CTI. (Drag and then press Shift to snap the final Transition Completion keyframe to the CTI.)

Altering the linear wipe to work with the new text

Save your work, and close the composition.

The purple section

You're almost finished with the main sequences: You just need to take care of your friend Purple. Although the layout of the purple moving squares background is more similar to the original orange section, you want to reuse the photo cross fade you created in the green section:

1   Duplicate the Section2_Green comp, and rename it Section3_Purple. Open the Section3_Purple composition.

2   Select the Green Squares layer. To replace this layer but retain its keyframes, press Alt (Windows) or Option (Mac OS) as you drag the Purple Squares composition from the Project window onto the Green Squares layer.

3   At time 0;00, change the Position keyframe on the Purple Squares layer to 154, 456.

4   At time 1;29, change the Position keyframe to 124, 110.

Leave the keyframes at time 0;25 and time 1;06, because they hold the transition.

5   Select the Moving BG Green layer. Hold down Alt (Windows) or Option (Mac OS), and drag the Moving BG Purple composition onto it to replace it.

6   Move the Moving BG Purple layer to Position 355, 326.

7   Change the BG Green layer's name to BG Purple, and change the color to pale purple (RGB: 187, 168, 255).

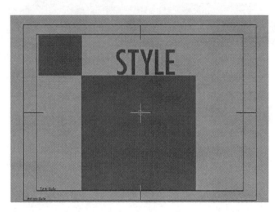

Changing the layout and colors for the purple section

The Vertical Bar and Horizontal Bar must be moved, sized, and colored to match the new layout:

1   Go to time 4;10. Change the color of the Vertical Bar layer to RGB 214, 209, 255 and its dimensions to 116 × 540.

2   Move the layer to Position 137, 329.

3   Change the Horizontal Bar layer's color to 214, 209, 255 and its dimensions to 720 × 115.

4   Move the layer to Position 442, 113.

The pictures must also be replaced, and you need to move the matte in relation to the new backdrop:

1   Select the Chandelier layer, and then hold down Alt (Windows) or Option (Mac OS) while dragging **Chair_02.jpg** onto the layer in the Timeline.

2   Change the Scale to 60, 60% and the Position to 421, 310.

3   Select both Pic Matte layers, and set their Positions to 355, 280.

4   Select the Kitchen_02 layer, and then hold down Alt (Windows) or Option (Mac OS) while dragging **Television.jpg** onto it in the Timeline.

5   Change the layer's Scale to 50, 50%, and move it to Position 360, 271.

Adjusting the mattes and pics to work with the new layout

Naturally, the text elements also need to change for the purple section:

1   Change the STYLE text layer's color to darkest purple (RGB: 85, 60, 168).

2   Move the layer to Position 354, 477 so it's below the photo.

3   Change the SPACE text layer to read *FORM*.

4   Change the layer's color to darkest purple (RGB: 85, 60, 168).

5   Set the layer's Position to 138, 298.

6   Change the LIGHT text layer to read *FUNCTION*.

7   Change the color to a really dark purple (RGB: 85, 60, 168), and set the Position to 353.5, 126.5.

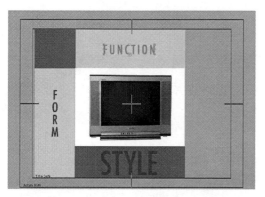

Changing the text for the purple section

For some variety, swap the In points of the FUNCTION and FORM layers:

1   Go to the In point of the FORM layer (time 5;18), and set a new composition marker (Shift+3).

2   Go to the In point of the FUNCTION layer (time 4;13).

3   Select the FORM layer, and press the [key to move the In point to the current time.

4   Press 3 to return to the composition marker at time 5;18.

5   Select the FUNCTION layer, and press [to move its In point.

Switching the timing on the horizontal and vertical text

Looks good—but it's a little too boxed in comparison to the green and orange sections, which use the small square solid to break up the square shape the other elements create. Never fear, though; there is a simple solution:

•   At time 4;10, set the Transition Completion keyframes for both the Horizontal Bar and the Vertical Bar layers to 0% so the solids extend beyond the screen.

Settings for the Linear Wipe effect

Save your work, and close the composition.

The yellow section

You're almost finished creating your sections. Now you'll add the logo with a new twist on the end tag that you created in the previous chapter.

Create a new composition named Section4_Yellow in the **Sections** folder, with dimensions 720 × 540, Frame Rate 29.97, and Duration 10;00. Although you could copy and replace the footage you need and delete the rest, it's just as fast to build this comp from scratch:

1 Drag the Yellow Squares composition to the Timeline at time 0;00, and then turn on the Collapse Transformations switch.

2 At time 0;00, create a Position keyframe of 132, 114.

3 At time 0;25, change the Position to 360, 270.

4 Go forward three frames to time 0;28. Create a new solid named Yellow BG that's comp size and pale yellow (RGB: 252, 253, 162).

5 Drag the Yellow BG layer under the Yellow Squares layer in the Timeline.

6 Go to time 2;00, and add the Style_Logo composition above the other two layers in the Timeline.

7 Insert a 0% Opacity keyframe.

8 Go to time 2;10, and change the Opacity to 100%.

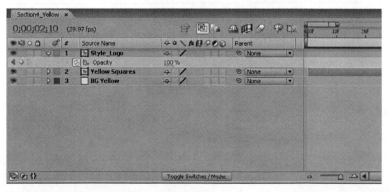

Beginning to build the yellow section

Save and preview your work.

Completing the end tag

Now you'll add the company's Web address and animate the text's tracking so the text expands onto the screen:

1 Return to the Section4_Yellow comp, and go to time 3;00.

2 Create a new text layer that says *www.styledesigncenter.com*.

3 Position the layer so it's centered below the logo.

4 Add a 0% Opacity keyframe.

5 Go forward 15 frames to time 3;15, and change the Opacity to 100%.

6 Press the J key to go back to time 3;00.

7 Display the text properties for the layer, and then choose Animate > Tracking in the Timeline.

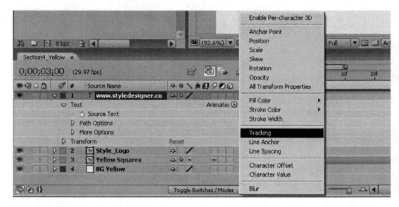

The Animate menu in the Timeline

8 Add a Tracking Amount keyframe, and set it to −20 to squish the letters together.

9 Go to time 3;15, and change the Tracking Amount to 5.

Save and preview your work. After the bevel effect covers the logo, the Web address expands outward to the comp edges.

Finishing Touches

You're undoubtedly ready to see all this hard work in action. Now you can assemble the final spot with each of the sections. This will take practically no time at all:

- Create a new composition named Squares2_Final with dimensions 720 × 540, Frame Rate 29.97, and Duration 30:00.

- At time 0;00, add Section1_Orange to the Timeline.

- Go to time 7;00, and add Section2_Green to the Timeline.

- Go to time 14;15, and add Section3_Purple to the Timeline.

- Go to time 22;00, and add Section4_Yellow to the Timeline.

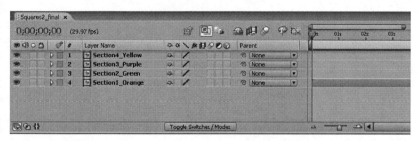

The finished Timeline

Now Try This

Well done: You've finished your second spot for the Style Design Center. By adding 3D space to the solids, you can really grab the viewer's attention and create a slick, hip, graphic look that has a sense of depth.

- For those who really like a challenge, play with shrinking the Square 1 on the Moving BG. Then add the smaller square on each point. Replace the smaller solids and the images with video clips. Now you have one large screen displaying video, surrounded by four smaller screens simultaneously showing clips.

CHAPTER 3 | Designing Title Effects

You don't need to search in any particular area for ideas for titles and credits; if you keep your eyes and mind open, ideas can be found everywhere from movie trailers to cereal boxes to the night sky. You can also get ideas by first designing something you might consider conventional and then working to transform it from there. That's what you'll do with the project in this chapter.

One common approach to bringing text onto the screen is to have it fade in as a blur and then come into focus once the text reaches its final destination. You'll use that approach as the basis for the main title in this chapter's project. But you'll customize the technique by using shooting stars and light flashes to introduce each section of the title.

It Works Like This

Check out the **Ch3_Finished_Movie.mov** file on the CD to see the text effects you'll create in this chapter. You'll animate the text onto the screen with a blurred motion, revealing one section at a time with light bursts. Here are the project's basic steps:

1. Create a background blur for the title.

2. Divide the title into sections by using masks, and then animate each mask's opacity.

3. Use the Lens Flare effect on a solid to create flashes that reveal each section of the title.

4. Create "comets" by animating a masked and feathered solid.

A comet-like solid and light flash introducing sections of the title

The blurred title, fully revealed

Preparing to Work

To prepare for this project, do the following:

1   Start with a new project, and import the **BackgroundMovie.mov** file from this chapter's folder on the book's CD.

2   Save your project as Ch 3 Title Effects.

Creating the Title

This movie is built within a single composition, which you'll create now:

1   Create a new comp named Master Comp, using the Web Video, 320 × 240 preset, with Frame Rate 30 and Duration 10;00 seconds.

2   Select the Title-Action Safe button at the bottom of the Comp window.

3   Click the Horizontal Type tool in the Tools palette, and set the following properties in the Character and Paragraph palettes:

>   Fill Color: white
>
>   Stroke Color: None
>
>   Font Family: Myriad
>
>   Font style: Roman
>
>   Font size: 40 pixels
>
>   Tracking: −50
>
>   Centered text

Your text will be big enough to be read easily, but these settings leave enough room around the title so that a background and other animated elements can also be viewed.

4   Press Ctrl+Alt+Shift+T (Windows) or Opt+Command+T (Mac OS) to create a new text layer in the center of the Comp window. Then, type the title **LA HI-RISE**.

5   Select the layer in the Timeline, and press the up arrow key several times to nudge the layer upward to make room for a second line of text underneath.

We used all caps so that the tall letters keep the high-rise theme of the title and project.

The title

Dividing the Title

You may have noticed that in After Effects, there are several ways to accomplish the same result. When you're deciding which technique is best, it often comes down to personal preference and work style. Sometimes the best technique is the one that can be most easily revised when your client wants you to tweak things here and there.

The objective in the next few steps is to reveal sections of the LA HI-RISE title at different times. One way to accomplish this is to duplicate the text layer and apply a separate mask to each text layer while staggering the start time for each layer. You can also create a separate text layer for each group of letters and then animate the layers separately. In this project you'll use only one layer to do this, because it takes fewer system resources and allows previews to play back more quickly:

1   Go to time 1;00, and use the Rectangular Mask tool to draw a mask around the letter *L* in the Master Comp window.

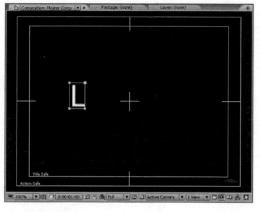

Masking the letter L

2   Continue using the Rectangular Mask tool to create masks for the letter *A*, the letters *HI*, the hyphen with the letters *RI*, and the letters SE, for a total of five masks. When you're placing the masks, be sure you cover each letter or set of letters completely and don't overlap the adjoining letters. To get a closer look at your masks and letters, press Ctrl (Windows) or Command (Mac OS) and the plus-sign key (+) to increase the magnification of the Composition window.

Masking the title

3   To make each mask easier to identify in the Timeline, click the mask's name, press Enter or Return, and then type the letter or letters that are masked. Repeat this for each mask.

The renamed masks in the Timeline

Animating the Masks

Now you'll animate the Mask Opacity of each mask and reveal the letters at different times:

1   Select all the masks, and press TT to display each mask's Mask Opacity property.

2   Go to time 1;00, and set a 0% Mask Opacity keyframe for mask L.

3   Go forward one frame to time 1;01, and change the Mask Opacity value to 100%.

Animating mask L's Mask Opacity

4   Select both Mask Opacity keyframes, and copy them.

5   Go forward 19 frames to time 1;20, select mask SE, and paste the keyframes.

6   Go forward 20 frames to time 2;10, select mask HI, and paste the keyframes.

7   Go forward 20 frames to time 3;00, select mask A, and paste the keyframes.

8   Go forward 20 frames to time 3;20, select mask –RI, and paste the keyframes.

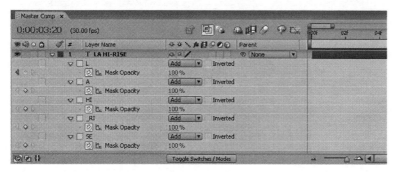

All the Mask Opacity keyframes in place

Press Home and then the spacebar to preview the animation. You should see the masked sections of the title appear at different times.

Creating the Title Blur

It's time to duplicate the text layer and use it to create the blurred title that appears before the main title comes into focus:

1   Select the LA HI-RISE layer, and duplicate it.

2   Select the lower LA HI-RISE layer in the Timeline, apply Effect > Blur & Sharpen > Fast Blur, and set Blurriness to 10. (No keyframe is needed.)

3   To make the topmost text layer appear after the blurred version fades in, go to time 3;20 and add a 0% Opacity keyframe to the top layer.

4   Press Alt + [(Windows) or Opt + [(Mac OS) to trim the layer's In point and leave its keyframe at the current point in time. (If you press only [, the keyframe moves to time 7;20, which you don't want to happen.)

Trimming layer 1 without moving its keyframe

5   Go to time 5;00, and change the layer's Opacity to 100%.

If you preview the animation, the blurred letters should fade in at different times. Then the sharp version of the title should quickly fade in on top of the blurred letters.

Adding Flashes of Light

You'll create light flashes by animating the Lens Flare effect (available only in the Professional version of After Effects). First, you'll create a Flare Center keyframe over each portion of the title at the same time each portion is revealed. Then, you'll move the flare forward a bit in time so that viewers see the flash just before they see the title come into view.

Note: If you have the Standard version of After Effects (and so don't have the Lens Flare effect), you may be able to create similar results by importing a Photoshop file that uses the Photoshop Lens Flare filter. It won't be nearly as easy to work with as the After Effects effect, but it's worth a try.

---

1 Go to time 0:00, and create a new comp-size solid named Light Flash that's colored black (RGB: 0, 0, 0).

Settings for the Light Flash solid

2 Apply Effect > Generate > Lens Flare to the solid. It's a bit too brilliant right now, but you'll tone it down later.

3 Display the Modes column in the Timeline, and set the Light Flash layer's mode to Screen. Doing so lets you reveal the text layers behind the black solid in the next steps.

Blending the Light Flash layer with the title

4 Go to time 1;01, and create a keyframe for the effect's Flare Center property. Press U to reveal the Light Flash layer's keyframes in the Timeline.

5 Reposition the Flare Center so that it lies right over the blurred *L* in the Comp window. The light will act as a reveal for the blurred text layer later in the project.

6 Go to time 1;21, and drag the icon in the Flare Center over the next portion of the title (the letters *SE*) that's revealed in the Comp window. Be sure to drag the circled + (plus sign) at the center of the flare; otherwise, a keyframe isn't created when you reposition the lens flare.

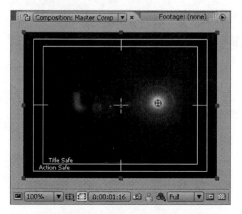

Animating the lens flare's center

7   Repeat step 6 at times 2;11 (letters *HI*), 3;01 (*A*), and 3;21 (*-RI*).

Next, we'll show you an easy way to offset the time of all five Flare Center keyframes:

1   Go to time 0;26, and click the Flare Center property name to select all of its keyframes.

2   Hold down your mouse pointer on the first keyframe, press Shift, and drag to snap the first keyframe to the Current Time Indicator (CTI). Reposition all the keyframes accordingly.

If you preview the comp at this point, the lens flare should glide back and forth over the title. The masked sections of the title fade in right after the lens flare passes over a section.

Now you'll make the lens flare stay put over each set of letters until the next set appears, instead of gliding between the letters:

1   Make certain that all your Flare Center keyframes are selected.

2   Choose Animation > Toggle Hold Keyframe. This option prevents interpolation between the keyframes so the property's value doesn't change until the next keyframe.

Setting the Flare Center keyframes' interpolation to Hold

Animating the Flare Brightness

Next, you'll animate the flare's brightness so that it fades in and out when it reveals each section of the title:

1   Go to time 0;26, and add a keyframe to the Lens Flare effect for 0% Flare Brightness.

2   Move forward five frames to time 1;01, and change the Flare Brightness to 85%.

3   Move forward five more frames to time 1;06, and change Flare Brightness back to 0%. These keyframes make the first flare fade in and out.

4   Click the Flare Brightness property name to select all three keyframes. Copy them, and then paste them at the same point in time as each Flare Center keyframe (1;16, 2;06, 2;26, and 3;16).

Pasting the Flare Brightness keyframes

At this point, your lens flare should fade in to reveal each portion of the title and then fade out.

Creating the Comets

You have your light flashes; now you need to add the shooting-star or comet effect that coincides with each light flash. Each comet is made by animating a solid that's shaped by feathered masks:

1 Go to time 0;26, and create a white solid layer named White Line that's 200 × 50. The final line won't be nearly that large, but this size gives you room to feather the layer masks you'll add next.

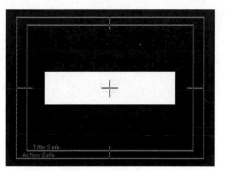

Creating the first White Line solid layer

2 Use the Rectangular Mask tool (Q) to create a thin straight line within the solid. Be sure areas of the solid surround all four sides of the mask for feathering.

3 Press F on the keyboard to display the Mask Feather property in the Timeline, and set its value to 3, 3.

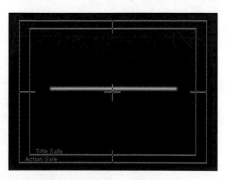

A feathered rectangular mask makes the comet trail.

4 To add a small comet head, use the Elliptical Mask tool (Q) to draw an oval shape near the left end of the new line.

5 Set the oval mask's Mask Feather to 10, 10.

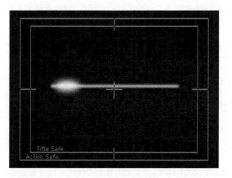

Adding a comet head by using the Elliptical Mask tool

Now you can animate the comet:

1 Turn on the lock next to each mask. Then, go to time to 1;01, where the first flash appears.

2 Line up the oval portion of the white line with the bright spot in the lens flare, and add a Position keyframe to the White Line layer.

3 Back up to time 0;26. To keep the line straight as it moves, hold down Shift while you move the White Line layer off the screen to the right.

4 To complete the cycle, go to time 1;06, and move the line off the screen to the left while pressing the Shift key.

The line should now zip across the screen, and the comet head should line up with the light flash. If you need to refine the size of the line, try changing only the y value of the solid layer's Scale property to thin the line and maintain its proportion relative to the feather.

Tip: You may have noticed that the Position velocity (the speed of the animation for the Position parameter) isn't even from start to finish. If you want to make the line travel at the same speed throughout the animation, expand the Position property in the Timeline, and deselect the box under the middle keyframe to make it a roving keyframe. Doing so makes the middle keyframe interpolate its speed from the previous and next keyframes.

Now that you've created one flying comet, you'll create duplicates of it and align the copies' timing with the other lens flares:

1   Select the Light Flash layer, and press U to reveal its keyframes.

2   Duplicate the White Line layer. Move the In point of the new White Line layer to time 1;16 so that it lines up with the start of the second set of the three Lens Flare keyframes.

3   Repeat step 2 three more times to create the remaining three lines, but align the In point of the new lines with the start of the other sets of Flare Brightness keyframes at times 2;06, 2;26, and 3;16.

Aligning the remaining lines

Press Home and then the spacebar to preview the animation. A comet should fly across the Comp window from right to left, and a flare should fade in and out to reveal each set of letters in the title.

Stretching the Title

There's just one last animation to complete before this section of the project is finished!

1   Go to time 5;00. Select the LA HI-RISE text layers, press S to display their Scale properties, and add a 100, 100% Scale keyframe to each layer.

2   Go to time 9;29, and change the Scale property for both layers to 130, 100%. This will slowly expand the title horizontally, similar to a tracking effect.

Now Try This

Try some of the following steps to create a suitable background for the animation and to add the remaining elements seen in this chapter's sample movie:

- Create a white solid that's the same size as the composition, and use the Rectangular Mask tool in Subtract mode to make the project's white letterbox.

- Add symbols that represent city life, and scroll them across the bottom of the screen. We used the Webdings font to create these in the project's sample movie, and we applied blending modes to integrate them into the background.

- Add the background movie from the **Chapter 03** folder on the book's CD, and add Blur and Levels effects to it to enhance its impact. Apply a Drop Shadow effect to the topmost LA HI-RISE text layer to give a sense of depth.

CHAPTER 4 | Animated Columns

Animating columns and filling the columns with video or stills is a technique used in many contemporary television commercials and station IDs. They often start with a main picture that expands to the width of the screen; then columns of images randomly slide back and forth across the screen. It's an effective way to weave together different pieces of footage to create an animated collage–like portrait of a subject.

This chapter shows you some quick techniques for creating this complex and sophisticated look. You'll also discover how to create alternating layers of video that replace each other as the columns float over and under one another.

It Works Like This

Check out this chapter's final movie on this book's CD to see this project's end result. You'll discover how to create a collage of video that's replaced by other video as the footage moves via columns across the screen. The techniques are as follows:

1. Use a fast and automated method to put together sequences of footage and create transitions.

2. Create multiple animated masks to serve as windows on the footage.

3. Add transparency and richness to the scene by using a blending mode.

4. Use the new Box Blur effect.

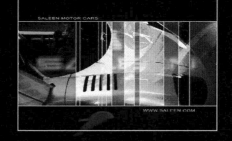

The main footage seen through masked windows

As the columns float across the main footage, other footage appears within the columns.

The company logo appears in the background as footage fades in and out inside the floating columns.

Preparing to Work

You'll configure all of this chapter's compositions for digital video by using one of the composition presets. The first comp you'll create contains the sequence of video footage that serves as the focal point of the entire project.

To prepare for this project, do the following:

1   Start with a new project, and save it as Ch4AnimatedColumns.

2   Import the **Footage** folder located in the Chapter 4 folder on the book's CD.

3   Import the **Saleen_logo_Layers.psd** file from this chapter's folder on the book's CD as footage with merged layers.

4   Create a new composition named Sequence Comp using the composition Preset NTSC DV, 720 × 480, and set the Duration to 10;00 seconds.

Project window with all your footage

Building the Car Sequence

The subject of this project's movie is a Saleen vehicle, which is featured in the ten pieces of footage you imported. In this section, you'll trim all that footage to the same duration, and then use a really quick method (just one step!) to distribute the footage across the Timeline and create a transition between the pieces:

1   Drag all ten Saleen_Car movies from the Project window into the Sequence Comp Timeline.

2   Go to time 2;00, select all the layers, and then press Alt +] (Windows OS) or Option +] (Mac OS) to trim the layers' Out point to the current time. (If you don't press Alt or Option, you'll move the layers' Duration bars instead of trimming them.)

Trimming the layers

You want each layer of footage to fade into the next sequentially, so you'll stagger the layers in time and add a transition between each pair.

3   Make sure all the layers are still selected, and are selected in order from Layer 1 to Layer 10. From the top of the application, choose Animation > Keyframe Assistant > Sequence Layers.

4 In the Sequence Layers dialog, check the Overlap box, set the Duration to 1;00 second, and set Transition to Dissolve Front Layer.

Settings for the Sequence Layers command

5 With all the layers still selected, press T on your keyboard to reveal their Opacity properties. Notice that Opacity keyframes were created for each layer to fade them out over a 1 second duration.

Click the Ram Preview button in the Time Controls palette to see the results. Each layer should play for a second and then fade away to display the next layer in the sequence.

With one step, all the layers are staggered and dissolve into one another.

Building the Layers

In this section, you'll assemble the master composition to contain all of the project's components (including the composition you made in the previous section). You'll also blend another piece of footage over the entire sequence that makes up the Sequence Comp and fade it in and then out of the composition:

1 Create a new composition named Master Comp using the NTSC DV, 720 × 480 preset, and set the Duration to 10;00 seconds.

2 Drag the Sequence Comp composition from the Project window to the Master Comp Timeline. Make sure the layer starts at time 0;00.

3 Drag the **Saleen_Car_01.avi** file from the Project window into the Timeline, above the Sequence Comp layer.

4 Change the Saleen_Car_01.avi layer's Blending Mode to Difference in the Modes column of the Timeline.

5 Press T to display the Saleen_Car_01.avi layer's Opacity, and add a 0% Opacity keyframe to the layer at time 0;00.

6 Go to time 1;00, and change the layer's Opacity to 100%.

7 Go to time 5;00, and add another 100% Opacity keyframe to the layer.

8 Press End to go to the end of the Timeline, and change the layer's Opacity to 0% to fade out the layer.

First stage of the Master Comp Timeline

Click the Ram Preview button in the Time Controls palette to view the results.

Building the Columns

It's time to create the animated masks that serve as sliding windows over the footage. To make it easier for you to keep track of which mask in the Timeline represents a mask in the composition, you'll turn on a preference that's new in After Effects 6.5:

1   Choose Edit > Preferences > User Interface Colors, and select Cycle Mask Colors.

Now, every time you draw a new mask, one of five colors will be used to identify the mask in the Timeline and in the Composition or Layer window. This will come in handy in the next section when you begin animating the masks.

2   Go to time 0;00, and double-click the Sequence Comp layer in the Master Comp Timeline to open it in a layer window. (Alternatively, you can complete this section in the Composition window; but the Layer window gives you more control.)

3   Click the Rectangular Mask tool in the Tools palette. Draw a vertical column starting below the bottom edge of the composition area and extending above the top edge of the composition.

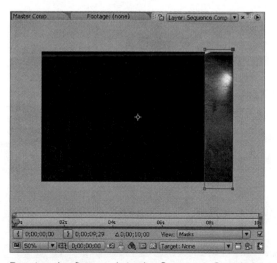

Drawing the first mask in the Sequence Comp's layer window

4   Draw four more columns that also span beyond the top and bottom edge of the comp. Place them in other areas of the composition, and make them varying widths.

Five masks with unique colors in the Sequence Comp layer

Animating the columns

Your next task is to animate the masks horizontally and randomly across the screen. You'll use each mask's Mask Path property as you would a Position property to animate its location over the Sequence Comp:

1   At time 0;00, expand the Sequence Comp in the Timeline, select all the masks, and then press M to display their Mask Path properties.

2   With all the masks still selected, click the stopwatch next to any Mask Path property to add a keyframe to all the masks.

3   Go to time 2;00, and click Mask 1's name in the Timeline to select the mask.

4   Using the Selection tool, drag Mask 1 to the opposite side of the comp.

5   Move the other four masks to new locations on the layer.

Tip: Remember to select the mask's name in the Timeline first in order to select all four vertices before moving the mask. Otherwise, you'll reshape the mask instead of moving it.

6   Go to time 4;00, and again move each mask to a new location.

7   Select the Mask Path keyframes for all five masks, and copy them.

8   Go to time 6;00, and paste the keyframes.

Pasting all the Mask Path keyframes

9   To add some definition to the boundaries of the masked areas, go to the Master Comp Timeline, select the Sequence Comp layer, and choose Effect > Generate > Stroke.

10 Check the All Masks option in the Effect Controls window, and set Color to white (RGB: 255, 255, 255). Now each mask has a white outline.

Settings for the Stroke effect in the Effect Controls window

Branding the Project

You've assembled the footage and animated its masks. Now it's time to add the logo, which is a Photoshop file. You'll set the logo behind the footage so that it teases the viewers by allowing them to see bits of the logo between the masks but never the entire thing:

1   Go to time 0;00 in the Master Comp Timeline, and drag the **Saleen_logo_layers.psd** file from the Project window to the Timeline below the Sequence Comp layer.

2   Duplicate the Saleen_logo_Layers layer, and add a 0% Opacity keyframe to both logo layers.

3   Go to time 3;00, and change both layers' Opacity to 100%.

4   Go to time 7;00, and add another 100% Opacity keyframe to both layers.

5   Go to time 9;00, select only the bottommost logo layer (layer 4), and change the layer's Opacity to 0%.

Now parts of the logo appear as the masks move back and forth over the footage.

Animating and revealing the logo

So far you've set up the logo to only play peek-a-boo with the user, by hiding it behind the footage. Next you'll fade out the footage at the end of the project to reveal the entire logo. You'll also give the logo more life by stretching it over time and adding a halo look to it:

1   Go to time 6;00, and add a 100% Opacity keyframe to the Sequence Comp layer.

2   Go to time 7;00, and change the layer's Opacity to 0%. Now the logo is fully visible.

3   Go to time 0;00, add a Scale keyframe to both logo layers, and set both keyframes to 85, 85%.

4   Press the End key to go to the end of the Timeline (time 9;29). Change layer 3's Scale to 100, 100% and layer 4's Scale to 150, 150%.

5   Select layer 4, and choose Effect > Blur & Sharpen >Box Blur. Set Iterations to 3 and Blur Radius to 10 in the Effect Controls window.

Save the project, and preview your results.

Settings for the Box Blur effect in the Effect Controls window

The logo, fully revealed

Tip: If you often use the same group of settings (or nearly the same) when you use a particular effect, then save that effect with those settings as a preset. To create the preset, set up the effect's settings as you want them, go to the Effect Controls window, and choose Save Selection As Animation Preset from the Animation Presets menu. (Despite the name Animation Preset, animation isn't required.) One way to then use your preset is to apply the effect as you normally would and choose your preset's name from the Animation Presets menu in the Effect Controls window.

Now Try This

Here's a series of steps to bring more attention to the car's logo and add more pizzazz:

1 Create a new comp named Letter Box that uses the same comp preset you've been using, with Duration set to 10;00 seconds.

2 Drag the Master Comp from the Project window into the Letter Box Timeline, starting at time 0;00.

3 Use the Rectangular Mask tool in Add mode to mask over the Master Comp in a format that looks like a 16:9 letterbox.

4 Apply the Stroke effect to the mask.

5 Use the new Text Animation Presets to animate titles in the top and bottom black areas of the screen, above and below the new stroke lines.

6 Use Opacity keyframes to create a 15-frame fade up of the Master Comp layer.

CHAPTER 5 | Unscrambling Type

When you're designing titles and credits, it's a challenge to capture the audience's attention and get them to read the text. I recently created a segment open for a network TV show in which I animated letters that spelled a sitcom character's name, scrambled into nonsense, and then unscrambled to reveal the name of the actor portraying the character. Scrambled words that gradually unscramble can help keep people engaged as they try to figure out what words are forming.

After this project is completed, you'll know how to animate text to unscramble itself. In addition, you'll animate text in 3D space and create a northern lights effect behind the text.

It Works Like This

To see what you'll design with this project, check out the **Ch5FinishedProject.mov** file in this chapter's folder in the book's CD. In this chapter, you'll create a promo for an electronic exposition at a local convention center. In the process, you'll do the following:

1. Unscramble text using the Character Offset animator to reveal the title.

2. Animate text in 3D space to bring the text in, rotate it, and send it out of the scene.

3. Add a provided background movie and apply a Box Blur effect to it.

4. Create an atmospheric multicolored ghosting effect behind the text.

The first layer of scrambling text comes in from above.

The first word unscrambles while the next word scrambles in.

After all four words unscramble, the layers rotate and separate in space.

Preparing to Work

To prepare for this project, do the following:

1   Start with a new project, and save it as Ch5ScrambledText.

2   Import the **Background.mov** file from this chapter's folder on this book's CD.

3   Create a new composition named Random Text Basic using NTSC D1, Square Pix 720 × 540 with Duration 5;00 seconds.

4   Turn on the Title-Action Safe button at the bottom of the Comp window to display the boundaries outside of which text might be cut off by particular displays.

Creating the Words

You always need to consider the overall look and feel of the elements (font style, background choices, and so on) in any project, to make certain they're appropriate for the project's destination. For example, readability is an important consideration when you're choosing fonts and colors. Some fonts look great and read well when displayed on a computer, television, or printed page but become more difficult to read when they're animated.

Create the title for this project with the following steps:

1   Select the Horizontal Type tool, and set the following properties in the Character and Paragraph palettes:

>   Font Family: Century Gothic or a font that looks similar to the title text in the final project's movie
>
>   Size: 48 pixels
>
>   Fill Color: green (RGB: 0, 255, 0)
>
>   Alignment: Center Text

Tip: Double-click a text layer in the Timeline to select the text, and click the font family name in the Character palette (instead of the pop-up menu arrow). Then you can use the up and down arrow keys on your keyboard to go through the fonts one by one while viewing each font's appearance in the Composition window. You can also press a letter to jump to the fonts whose names begin with that letter.

Settings for the Text layers

2   Type the word **CYBER** in uppercase in the Composition window, and then either press the Enter key on the numeric keypad or click the Selection tool in the Tools palette to get out of text-entry mode.

3 Create three more text layers for the words *WORLD,*
   ELECTRONIC, and *EXPOSITION.* You can put them anywhere in
   the composition for now; you'll reposition them in the next section.

Four separate text layers in temporary locations

Random Text Basic composition's Timeline

Positioning the Text in 3D

In the next few steps, you'll set up the position each text layer will assume
after it flies in through 3D space from behind the user:

1 Select all the text layers in the Timeline, turn on their 3D switches in
   the Switches column, and then press P on your keyboard to display
   their Position properties.

2 With all the layers still selected, change their X Position values to 360
   and their Z values to 0.0.

3 Deselect the layers. Click the Y Position value for the each layer, and
   enter the following value listed for that layer. Press Tab (to go forward)
   and Shift+Tab (to go backward) to navigate through the Position
   values in a layer and to the next layer's values:

   EXPOSITION: 380

   ELECTRONIC: 320

   WORLD: 260

   CYBER: 200

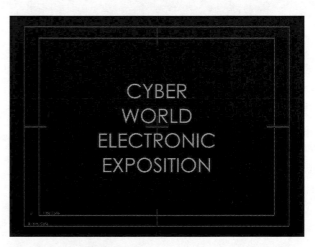

Position values for each text layer

The title's landing position

Randomizing the Text

You'll animate the type using the powerful Animator features, which are only available for text layers—in this case, you'll use the animator to scramble the letters with the Character Offset property:

1   Press Home on your keyboard to go to time 0;00.

2   Select all the layers, and press UU to display the Text and Transform property groups.

3   In the EXPOSITION layer, click the arrow to the right of the word *Animate* to display that menu, and then choose Character Offset.

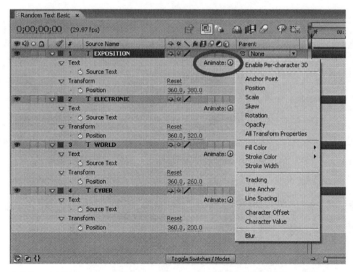

Adding a Character Offset animator to the EXPOSITION text layer

4   Add a keyframe to the Character Offset property, still at time 0;00, and set it to 40.

5   Go to time 0;15, and change the Character Offset value to 0.

6   Click the Animator 1 name to select the entire animator, and then copy it.

7   Press Home to return to time 0;00, select the other three layers, and paste. An Animator 1 and two Character Offset keyframes will appear in each layer's Text property group in the Timeline.

Timeline with Character Offset keyframes in place

How does your text look at time 0;00? It should be an unintelligible mess, thanks to the character-offset settings you applied to the layers. With a Character Offset value of 40, the original letters are each replaced by whatever letter exists 40 letters forward alphabetically. For example, 40 letters forward from the letter C is the letter Q. (Since there are only 26 letters in the alphabet, you must start over at letter A once you hit Z, in order to figure out the letter that will display.) If you go time 0;14, where the Character Offset should already be set to 3, you'll see that every letter is 3 characters away from the letters in the original title.

At time 0;14 seconds, Character Offset is 3, so the letters shown are three letters forward from the original title's letters.

Staggered text layers

Staggering the Text

Next, you need to stagger the start time of the layers so they arrive in the comp one at a time:

1   Display the In column in the Timeline, and then set the value of each layer's In point as shown here:

   EXPOSITION: 2;00

   ELECTRONIC: 1;15

   WORLD: 1;00

   CYBER: 0;15

2   Close the In column in the Timeline.

Press Home and then the Spacebar to view the results so far. You should see a scrambling word appear; as soon as the word unscrambles itself, the next scrambling word in the title appears.

Making 3D Look Easy

In this section, you'll use a Null Object layer to simplify animating the layers in 3D space. Currently, the project just generates letters that unscramble. The following steps add some depth and dynamism to the effect. You'll parent the text layers to the null object to perfectly synchronize the text by animating one layer (the null object) and maintain the positional relationships.

Follow these steps:

1   With the Random Text Basic composition open, choose View > New View to open a second window for the comp.

2   Set the second Comp window's 3D View pop-up menu to Top so you can see the results of the changes you make in the following steps.

3   Choose Layer > New > Null Object.

4   Turn on the 3D switch for the Null 1 layer in the Switches column. In its default position at 360, 270, 0, you can see the square outline of the entire null object overlapping the words *ELECTRONIC* and *EXPOSITION* in the Comp window.

5   Add a Position keyframe to the Null 1 layer at time 0;00, and set the keyframe to 360, 270, -890. Negative Z values move the Null 1 layer toward the viewer, so now you can only see the null object's upper-left corner.

6   Go to time 2;15, and change the Position to 360, 270, 0. Now the Null 1 layer moves away from the viewer from time 0;00 to 2;15 and lands in the same point along the Z axis as the text layers.

7   Still at time 2;15, add a keyframe to the null layer's Orientation, and set it to 0.0, 300, 0.0. Notice how the null object is now angled away from the viewer in both comp views.

8   Go to time 4;00, and add another Position keyframe with the same value (360, 270, 0) as the keyframe at time 2;15.

9   At time 4;00, change the orientation to 0.0, 0.0, 0.0.

10   Go to time 4;29, and change the Position to 360, 270, -1020. This negative value for Z puts the null object out of view behind the viewer.

11   Go to time 2:15, and lock the null layer.

12   Select all the layers except the Null 1 layer, and display the Parent column in the Timeline.

13   Choose Null 1 from the Parent menu adjacent to any selected layer in the Timeline to set the value for all the selected layers.

Assigning the null object as the parent of the other layers

14   With all the text layers still selected at time 2;15, add a Position keyframe to each of them.

15   Deselect the layers, go to time 4;00, and change the layers' Position values as follows:

EXPOSITION: 0, 110, -200

ELECTRONIC: 0, 50, -100

WORLD: 0, -10, 0

CYBER: 0, -70, 100

Before you changed the layers' Positions, the layers all resided at the same point on the X and Z axes and differed only in the Y value. The changes in the Position values at time 4;00 create depth between the layers by separating them along the Z axis. Meanwhile, the layers rotate as they imitate the null object's orientation.

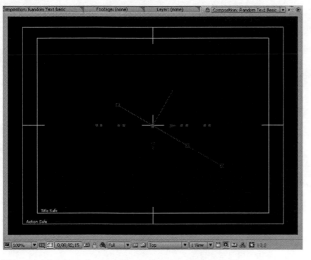

The text layers viewed from above at time 2;15

Select all your layers, drill them up, lock them down, and save the project. If you preview your work, the letters should unscramble as they fly into the scene, face the viewer unscrambled, turn counterclockwise by 30 degrees, and then fly at and beyond the viewer.

Adding an Atmospheric Background

Adding a background to this project gives the viewer a frame of reference for the text, which currently floats unanchored in 3D space. Lucky for you, we've provided the foundation for the background by giving you the **Background.mov** file, and you just need to add some finish to it:

1   Create a new composition with the same measurements as the other— NTSC D1 Square Pix, 720 × 540, with Duration 5;00—and name it Random Master Comp.

2   Drag the Random Text Basic composition from the Project window into the Random Master Comp Timeline at time 0;00.

3   To give the text a cloudy fill, apply Effect > Noise & Grain > Fractal Noise to the Random Text Basic layer. The effect's default settings are fine.

4   Drag the **Background.mov** file from the Project window to the Timeline at time 0;00, under the Random Text Basic layer.

5   Change the Background movie's Scale to 115, 115% to compensate for its dimensions, which are smaller than the composition. Because the background is a nonsquare pixel movie and the composition uses square pixels, there will be some distortion; but in this case, it will work to your advantage as a motion background.

6   Apply Effect > Adjust > Brightness & Contrast to the Background movie. Set the effect's Brightness to −70 and Contrast to 45.

7   Add a Box Blur effect with Blur Radius set to 15 and Blur Dimensions set to Vertical.

Creating the Text Lights

In this section, you'll add to the background by duplicating the existing text layer, animating the new layer, and changing it to a supplemental shadow. You can easily do this using a only a few additional effects:

1 Duplicate the Random Text Basic layer, and rename layer 2 Fill Text.

2 Change the Fill Text layer's Scale to 150, 150%.

3 Apply Effect > Blur & Sharpen > Box Blur, and set the Blur Dimensions to Vertical and Iterations to 3.

4 Set a keyframe for a Blur Radius of 0 at time 0;00.

5 Go to time 2;15, and change Blur Radius to 55.

6 Expand the Fill Text layer's Fractal Noise effect, and change the effect's Blending Mode to Hue.

Now Try This

To add the remaining finishing touches that complete the look of this chapter's **Ch5FinishedProject.mov** movie file, do the following:

- Apply Effect > Perspective > Drop Shadow to the top text layer (Random Text Basic), and set the effect's Opacity to 85%, Direction to 282 degrees, Distance to 80, and Softness to 20.

- Create a letterbox, some supporting content, and a basic light zoom in just a few steps:

    1   At time 0:00, create a black, comp-size solid (720 × 540), and place it between the Random Text Basic layer and the Fill Text layer.

    2   Use the Rectangular Mask tool to draw over the center of the solid, and then change the mask's Mask Mode to Subtract.

    3   To outline the letterbox, apply a Stroke effect to it using the default effect values.

CHAPTER 6 | Station ID

If someone asked you how to add more depth to a scene in After Effects, you might first rattle off the names of several effects, such as any of the Perspective or Distort effects, or the various Emboss effects. Those work well to give depth to individual elements in a scene. But to give the entire scene more depth, you can add elements to the foreground or frame the scene to create the illusion.

This chapter's project uses a combination of both those methods to create a "deep" scene. To give you a running head start, the book's CD provides you with some video footage of a city landscape on top of which you can build your project. You'll create an animated iris or aperture to frame the scene and use effects to give the aperture its style and some substance. Finally, you'll use Zaxwerks' 3D Invigorator effect to extrude and animate a 2D drawing.

It Works Like This

Check out the **Ch6 Finished Project.mov** file in this chapter's folder on the book's CD to see the final results of this chapter's project. This project is created using only one composition and a few layers, yet the results contain a lot of depth and visual interest.

You'll use the following techniques:

1. Give footage of a cityscape a stylized night look with some effects.

2. Add a layer of scrolling text to the background.

3. Create an animated aperture that frames the city view.

4. Create a 3D object with the 3D Invigorator effect, a solid, and an Adobe Illustrator file.

The TV channel slowly spins in the center of the scene.

As the channels rotates, text scrolls upward.

Preparing to Work

You'll need to import a file and make sure a third-party effect is installed into After Effects in order to complete this chapter's project. The project uses some video footage, provided on the book's CD, to create the background. To create the 3D channel number 2, you'll use an Illustrator file and the Zaxwerks 3D Invigorator effect. You won't need to import the Illustrator file into your project, since the 3D Invigorator effect prompts you to open the Illustrator file from its actual location on your computer.

To prepare for this project, do the following:

1 Start with a new project, and save it as Ch6StationID.

2 Import the **City_Background.mov** file as footage from this chapter's folder on the book's CD.

3 Create a new composition named Master using the NTSC DV, 720 × 480 composition preset, with Duration 5;00 seconds.

Creating the Background

You'll create the background in three easy steps by importing your movie file and applying two effects to it. The Hue/Saturation effect helps give the footage a uniform appearance, and the Glow effect further stylizes the imagery:

1 Add the **City_Background.mov** file to the Master Timeline at time 0;00.

2 To give the City_Background.mov layer a blue hue, apply Effect > Color Correction > Hue/Saturation to the layer. Use these effect settings:

> Colorize (under Master Lightness): On
>
> Colorize Hue: 0 × 220
>
> Colorize Saturation: 45

Settings for the Hue/Saturation effect

3 To add some radiance to the city background, apply Effect > Stylize > Glow to the layer. Use these effect settings:

    Glow Threshold: 27%

    Glow Radius: 18

    Glow Intensity: 0.3

Settings for the Glow effect

The City_Background.mov layer with Hue/Saturation and Glow effects

Adding the Scrolling Text

A text layer that displays the names of 11 cities (presumably the news station's broadcasting area) scrolls upward on top of the city. To create this effect, you'll animate your text layer's Position property. Once you're done with this project, you can try using any of the Multi-Line text animation presets (in the Effects & Presets palette) to animate the layer instead.

Follow these steps:

1 Use these Settings for the Horizontal Type tool:

    Alignment: Center Text

    Font Family: Arial

    Text Size: 34px

    Leading: 72

    Tracking: 300

    Fill Color: White (RGB: 255, 255, 255)

    Stroke Color: None

Settings for the text layer

2 Type the names of 11 cities, with one city name per line, in a single text layer.

3 To set the starting position of the text layer, add a Position keyframe of 360, 505 at time 0;00. This keyframe starts the first line of text just outside the bottom edge of the composition and centered in the composition's width.

4   Press your keyboard's End key to go to time 4;29. Change the text layer's Position to 360, -725 to position the layer above the top edge of the Composition window.

The text's motion path starts below the composition and ends far above.

Save your project, and then preview your results. The text layer should now start offscreen at the bottom of the composition and scroll upward until every line of text is out of view.

Creating an Aperture

The city background is viewed through an aperture you'll create by masking two solid layers. You have a lot of freedom to make your aperture unique when you draw and position your masks; use our illustrations and masking instructions as a general guide. The solids' appearance is created with the Ramp and Bevel Alpha effects:

1   At time 0;00, create a comp-size Solid layer named Border 2 that's any color. Make sure the Solid layer is above the other layers in the Timeline.

2   Use the Elliptical Mask tool on the Solid layer to draw an oval shape that encompasses about two thirds of the composition. The right side of the mask in this chapter's final movie is within the composition, and the left side is out of view to the left of the composition. Use the illustration of the first iris as a guide.

3   Set the Mask's Mode to Subtract so you see the city through the oval shape.

Tip: Choose Layer > Mask > Free Transform Points after you select your mask in the Timeline to more easily move, rotate, and reshape your mask.

Making the first aperture

4   Still at time 0;00, add a Mask Shape keyframe to the Border 2 layer's mask.

5   Press End on your keyboard to go to time 4;29. Rotate and move the mask's shape up or down to a new location near the mask's current location, to create a slow and subtle movement.

Note: Make sure you move only the mask and not the Solid layer.

---

6   To create the second half of the iris, duplicate the Border 2 layer and rename the new layer Border 1.

7   At time 0;00, move the Border 1 mask so it encompasses the area opposite the Border 2 layer's mask. In this chapter's final movie, the left edge of the mask is within the composition, and the right edge is out of view on the right side.

8   At time 4:29, rotate and move the Border 1 mask up or down in the opposite direction of Border 2's mask.

The masked solids create a basic frame over the city scene.

Adding style to the aperture

Currently, your solids appear very flat, and their shapes appear to merge into one another (if you used the same fill color with each). You'll use the Ramp effect with unique settings for each solid so their colors are distinct from one another, and then you'll use the Bevel Alpha effect to give the solids some volume:

1   Select both Border layers, and apply Effect > Generate > Ramp to both.

2   To complement the blue hue in the city background, set the effect's Start Color to a yellow color and the End color to a blue color for one Border layer. Reverse the colors in the other Border layer's effect.

3   Select both Border layers, and apply Effect > Perspective > Bevel Alpha. Set the effect's properties as follows:

   Edge Thickness: 15

   Light Color: White (RGB: 255, 255, 255)

   Light Intensity: 0.70

4   Set the Bevel Alpha effect's Light Angle to 90 for the effect in Border 1 and to 0 in Border 2.

The Border layers using the Ramp and Bevel Alpha effects

Adding the News Channel

In this section, you'll create a 3D TV channel number by extruding an Illustrator file's shape from a Solid layer. You'll assign prebuilt surface textures and lighting to the object to quickly create the number's look. To make the number rotate in space, you'll animate a virtual camera instead of the number itself.

Note: If you don't already have the 3D Invigorator effect installed into After Effects, quit After Effects, and then install a trial version of the effect from the book's DVD.

Follow these steps:

1   At time 0;00, create a new comp-size Solid layer named 2, using any color.

2   Apply Effect > Zaxwerks > 3D Invigorator to the new solid. Choose "Open Illustrator File" on the menu, and then open the **2.ai** file from this chapter's folder on the book's DVD.

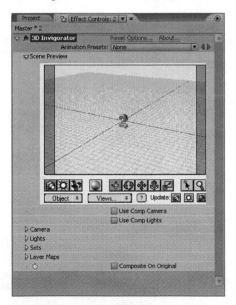

The 3D Invigorator effect's properties in the Effect Controls window

3   To assign a texture to the number, click Options in the upper-right corner of the Effect Controls window. Drag an object style onto the object in the Scene Preview area of the dialog, and click OK.

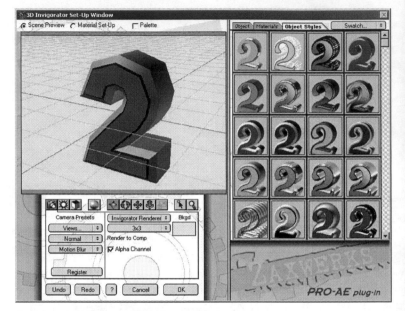

Applying the object style to the number

4   Expand the triangle next to the effect's Camera group in the Effect Controls window, add a keyframe to every property in the group, and set the camera properties as follows:

> Eye X: 300
>
> Eye Y: 500
>
> Eye Z: 500
>
> Target X: 0
>
> Target Y: 0
>
> Target Z: –15
>
> Distance: 907

Tumble Left: 116.29

Tumble Up: 22.21

Roll: 0

Ortho Size: 500

The camera's view with the 2 layer's first set of keyframes

5 Go to time 3;00, and change the effect's camera properties as follows:

Target Z: –10

Distance: 143.73

Tumble Left: –31.54

Tumble Up: 33.27

Ortho Size: 97.67

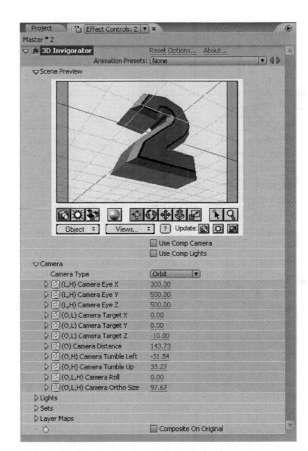

Animating the camera instead of the object

6   To assign a lighting style to the number, click Options in the upper-right corner of the Effect Controls window. Click the Light button (next to the Camera button), and then click the Lighting Styles tab in the right panel of the dialog. Drag a lighting style from the list onto the number in the scene preview area of the dialog, and click OK.

7   Apply Effect > Perspective > Drop Shadow to the layer named 2. Set the effect's Distance to 70 and Softness to 50.

Settings for the drop shadow

Save your project, and then preview your results. The number 2 should initially appear small and with its back to the viewer and then slowly rotate counter-clockwise as it moves closer to the viewer.

Adding Text to the Channel

The remaining finishing touch is to add the phrase *ON TUESDAY* in front of the channel number when the number comes to a stop at time 3;00:

1   Go to time 3;00, and create a text layer that displays *ON TUESDAY* above the 2 layer in the Timeline. Use these settings for the new text layer:

    Font Family: Arial Black

    Text Size: 18px

    Tracking: 300

    Fill Color: White (RGB: 255, 255, 255)

    Stroke Color: Red (RGB: 255, 0, 0)

    Stroke Width: 2px

    Stroke Style: Fill Over Stroke

2   Turn on the new text layer's 3D switch, and adjust the Position and Orientation values until the text lies on the front of the bottom stroke of the character and appears aligned with the front of the number.

Adding a phrase to the channel number

If you preview your animation, the words *ON TUESDAY* should appear at time 3;00.

Now Try This

At this point, your animation should look very similar to the finished movie in this chapter's folder on the book's CD, although your animation may have different colors and styles and the aperture may look different. Here are a number of suggestions that you can perform to refine this project even further:

- Select the individual Border layers, and animate the Light Angles of the Bevel Alpha effect to give the edges of the animated aperture more visual interest.

- Change the background text so that the names of the cities animate in alternating directions across the screen—some from right to left, and others from left to right.

- To really jazz up the scrolling text, remove the Position keyframes from the layer, and then apply a text animation preset from the Multi-Line category in the Effects & Presets palette to the layer. You can refine the resulting animation by tweaking the preset's settings in your Timeline. Press UU to reveal all the properties that were modified by the preset.

CHAPTER 7 | Heartbeat Car Commercial

The original idea for the heartbeat you'll visualize with this chapter's project was inspired by a project in which I set an oscilloscope waveform inside a logo. I really liked the idea and began to experiment with it as a means of expressing the excitement someone may feel the first time they drive a Saleen S7 car.

In this project, you'll learn how to use a variety of effects and a mask to create and animate the heartbeat. You'll also use effects to build a heart monitor to contain the heartbeat and to frame some video footage. The lessons you'll learn as you animate the heartbeat's path can be applied to other projects in which you want to animate lines and outlines.

It Works Like This

Check out the **Ch7 Saleen Heartbeat.mov** file in this chapter's folder on the book's CD to view the final results of this chapter's project. Video footage featuring a Saleen automobile serves as the background for the real star of this spot: an animated heartbeat. You'll learn to use combinations of effects and blending modes to create the layered look of the final project.

You'll use the following techniques:

1. Draw the path of a heartbeat with the Pen tool, and stroke the path with color.

2. Animate the heartbeat's path by animating the Stroke and Lens Flare effects.

3. Fade out the heartbeat's path by animating the Ramp effect and assigning a Track Matte to the heartbeat's layer.

4. Build a monitor for the heartbeat's path by using the Grid effect and an Adjustment layer.

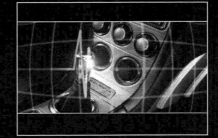

Video footage plays as the heartbeat goes across the screen.

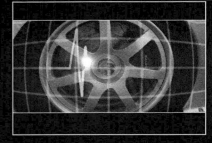

A ball of light leads the heartbeat's path across the screen.

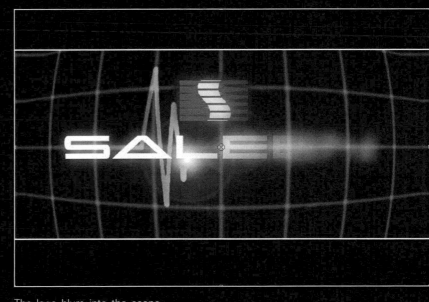

The logo blurs into the scene.

Preparing to Work

This project requires three movie files, an audio file, and a graphic still, all of which are provided on the book's CD. You need to import these items into your project and create your first composition before the real work begins.

To prepare for this project, do the following:

1 Start with a new project, and save it as Ch7HeartbeatCar.

2 Import the folders named **Audio, Footage,** and **Stills** from this chapter's folder on the book's CD. The **Footage** folder contains two AVI files and a MOV file, the **Stills** folder contains one PSD file, and the **Audio** folder contains one WAV file.

3 Create a new composition named Heartbeat using the NTSC DV, 720 × 480 comp preset, with Duration 1;00 second.

4 To keep your Project window organized, create a new folder named **Comps** and add the Heartbeat composition and all subsequent comps in this chapter to it.

The Project window

Creating the Heartbeat

You'll draw the heartbeat's path with the Pen tool by using the eyeball technique—that is, you'll draw the path by hand using an audio layer's waveform as your visual guide. As a result, your heartbeat path may not look exactly like the path in the illustrations or this chapter's finished movie; that's okay.

Follow these steps:

1 Add the **heartbeat.wav** file to the Timeline, and press your keyboard's L key twice to display the layer's audio track in the Timeline. You'll use the sound as a visual guide when drawing the path for the line in the heart monitor.

2 Create a new comp-size (720 × 480) Solid layer named Heartbeat, colored black (RGB: 0, 0, 0).

3 Use the Pen tool to draw a shape on the Heartbeat layer that resembles the waveform in the audio layer.

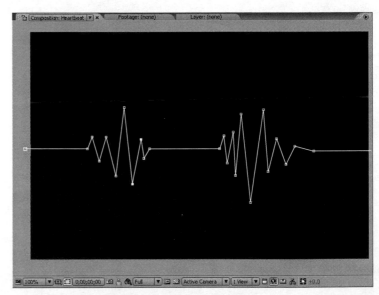

Drawing a heartbeat's path

4 Apply Effect > Generate > Stroke to the Heartbeat layer to outline the path. Set the effect's Color to bright green (RGB: 0, 255, 0) and the Brush Size to 3.0.

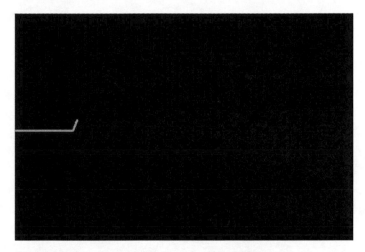

Stroking the heartbeat path

Animating the heartbeat

The Stroke effect has Start and End properties, which let you control the areas of a mask or path that are affected. If Start is set to 0% and End is set to 100% (or vice versa), then the entire path appears stroked. If both properties are set to the same value, then nothing is stroked. To animate the heartbeat's stroke so it moves from left to right, you'll animate the Stroke effect's End property in the following steps; you could just as easily animate the Start property with End set to 0%, instead, to get the same results. You'll use the eyeball technique again to get the right values for each keyframe:

1 Go to time 0;00, add a keyframe to the effect's End property, and change the property's value to 0%.

2 Go to the point in time that's just before the first spike in the audio layer's Waveform path, and scrub the Stroke effect's End value upward until the green stroke lies before the spikes in your mask's path.

After adding the Stroke effect's second End keyframe

3 Go to the point in time that's at the end of the first group of spikes in the audio layer's Waveform path, and then increase the End property's value until the stroke is at the end of the group of spikes in the mask.

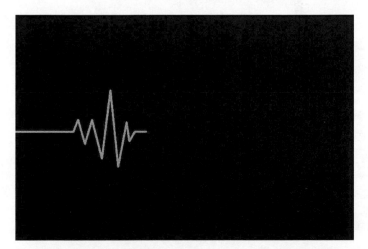

Completing the first heartbeat

4   Repeat steps 2 and 3 for the remaining spikes in the paths of the audio layer's Waveform and your mask.

5   Go the end of the Timeline, and set the End property to 100%.

6   To give the path some radiance, apply Effect > Stylize > Glow to the Heartbeat layer. Use these effect settings:

   Glow Threshold: 40%

   Glow Intensity: 2.0

   Color A (the inside color): Bright yellow (RGB: 255, 255, 0)

   Color B (the outside color): Bright green (RGB: 0, 255, 0)

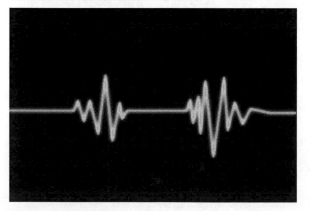

The Glow effect's settings in the Effect Controls window

The glowing heartbeat

Fading out the heartbeat

In this section, you'll use an easy technique to fade out the tail end of the heartbeat's stroked path as it moves from left to right, so it's more realistic. You'll animate a color gradient that's created with the Ramp effect and then use the layer as a Track Matte for the heartbeat's layer:

1   At time 0;00, create a new comp-sized Solid layer named Ramp that's any color. Place the layer above the other layers in the Heartbeat Timeline. (The solid's color will be overridden by the Ramp effect.)

2   Apply Effect > Generate > Ramp to the Ramp layer to create the gradients you'll need. Set the effect's Start of Ramp to 0, 240 and End of Ramp to 185, 240. These values fill most of the comp with white color that graduates to black on the left edge.

The Ramp effect's settings

The results of the Ramp effect and its settings at time 0;00

3   Set the Heartbeat layer's Track Matte to Luma Matte "Ramp", and
    press U on your keyboard to display the layer's keyframes

4   Go to the point in time where the Heartbeat layer's second keyframe
    lies, and add Start of Ramp and End of Ramp keyframes to the Ramp
    effect in the Ramp layer. Adjust the X value of the End of Ramp
    property until the End of Ramp marker (a circled plus sign) lies to the
    left of the rightmost point of the visible green stroke.

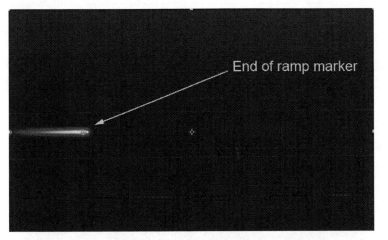

The End of Ramp marker should be to the left of the stroke's leading
point.

5   Go to the point in time where the Stroke effect's next keyframe lies,
    and increase the X value of the Ramp effect's End of Ramp property
    until it lies to the left of the stroke's leading point, so the rightmost
    point is fully revealed and the rest of it is fading out.

6   At the same point in time as the Stroke effect's fourth keyframe,
    repeat the previous step; but this time also increase the Start of Ramp
    property's X value so that you can't see most of the first heartbeat.

7   At the same point in time as the Stroke effect's fifth keyframe,
    increase the X value of the Ramp effect's End of Ramp property until
    it lies to the left of the stroke's leading point. Also increase the Start of
    Ramp property until you see only the last half of the second heartbeat.

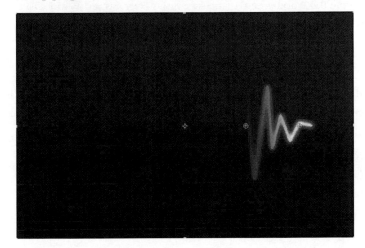

8   Press End to go to the end of the composition, and then increase the
    X values of the Start of Ramp and End of Ramp properties until you
    can't see the heartbeat's stroke.

The Heartbeat Timeline

Adding a ball of light

Next, you'll use the Lens Flare effect to create and animate a ball of white light that leads the stroked path across the screen. Follow these steps:

1   At time 0;00, add a new comp-size Solid layer named White Dot that's colored black (RGB: 0, 0, 0).

2   Apply Effect > Generate > Lens Flare to the White Dot layer, and set the effect's Flare Brightness to 70%.

3   Add a Flare Center keyframe to the effect, and set it to -50, 240. This starts the light offscreen.

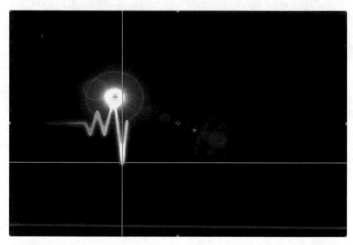

Settings for the Lens Flare effect at time 0;00

4   Set the White Dot layer's Blending Mode to Screen in the Timeline's Modes column. This lets the viewer see both the stroke and the lens flare.

5   Go to the point in time where the Heartbeat layer's second keyframe lies, and increase the Flare Center property's X value until the light ball is at the tip of the line stroke.

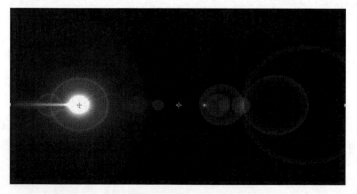

Aligning the Lens Flare to the stroke's leading point

6   Continue to move along the Timeline one frame at a time, and adjust the Flare Center property's position so that it always appear at the leading tip of the stroked path.

To position the Flare Center property, click the button that appears to the immediate left of the property's values in the Effect Controls window and then click in the Composition window where you want the Flare Center. Two white lines follow your mouse pointer to show you where the new point will be: where the lines intersect. Alternatively, you can drag the Flare Center icon in the Composition window to each new position. You can use the Page Up and Page Down keys to navigate along in time as you make the adjustments.

The place where the two white lines intersect defines the new position for the light flare.

Building the Heart Monitor

The style of the monitor enclosure you'll build to contain the heartbeat's path is like a relic from the earliest days of such devices. Before you build the monitor, you'll create a sequence of your heartbeat animation so that it loops continuously in the background. Here are the steps:

1 Create a new composition named Heart Monitor in your Project window's **Comps** folder, using the NTSC DV, 720 × 480 comp preset, with Duration 10;00 seconds.

2 Add the Heartbeat composition to the Heart Monitor Timeline at time 0;00.

3 Duplicate the Heartbeat layer nine times so you have a total of ten layers.

4 Select all the Heartbeat layers, and choose Animation > Keyframe Assistant > Sequence Layers. Make sure the Overlap option is unchecked and Transition is set to Dissolve Front Layer.

The Heartbeat Timeline after sequencing the layers

5 Create a new comp-size Solid layer named Grid that's any color. Make sure the layer is above all the other layers in the Timeline.

6 Apply Effect > Generate > Grid to the Grid layer, and set the effect's Border (grid line size) property to 2.5. Change the color to green.

7 To smooth out the grid lines, apply Effect > Blur & Sharpen > Fast Blur effect to the Grid layer, and set the effect's Blurriness property to 2.

Settings for the Grid layer's effects

8 To create a bulge in the virtual glass of your monitor, choose Layer > New > Adjustment Layer, and name the layer Bulge. Since an Adjustment layer only works on layers that are below it, make sure the layer is at the top of the Timeline.

9 Apply Effect > Distort > Bulge to the Bulge layer. Use these effect settings:

Horizontal Radius: 320

Vertical Radius: 320

Bulge Height: 0.7

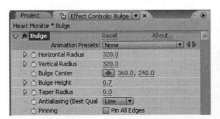

Settings for the adjustment layer's Bulge effect

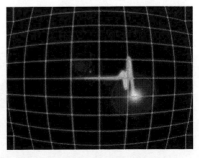

The Heart Monitor composition

Building the Movie Sequence

It's finally time to use the movie footage that you imported at the beginning of this project. All you need to do is put the movies in sequence, one after the other, and add transitions to them. You'll use the Sequence Layers command again, but with different options. Follow these steps:

1   Create a new composition named Car Movie in the **Comps** folder using the NTSC DV, 720 × 480 comp preset, with Duration 6;00 seconds.

2   Add the **Saleen_Car_02.avi, Saleen_Car_01.avi,** and **SaleenCar_04.mov** files to the Timeline at time 0;00. Saleen_Car_02 should be layer 1, Saleen_Car_01 should be layer 2, and Saleen_Car_04 should be layer 3.

3   Go to time 3;00, select all three layers, and press Alt-] (Windows) or Option-] (Mac OS) to trim the layers' Out points to the current time.

Trimming the Out points of the Saleen_Car layers

4   With the three layers still selected, choose Animation > Keyframe Assistant > Sequence Layers. Use these effect settings:

   Overlap: On

   Duration: 1;15

   Transition: Dissolve Front Layer

Press U on your keyboard to view the Opacity keyframes created by this command.

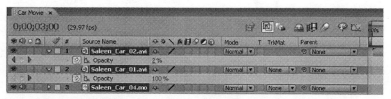

Viewing the sequenced layers

Putting It All Together

Now that all the major components are finished, you can assemble them into a master composition:

1   Create a new composition named Heartbeat Master in your **Comps** folder using the NTSC DV, 720 × 480 comp preset, with Duration 10;00 seconds.

2   Add the Heart Monitor composition to the Heartbeat Master Timeline at time 0;00.

3   To fade in the Heart Monitor layer, add a 0% Opacity keyframe at time 0;00 and a 100% Opacity keyframe at time 0;15.

4   To fade out the Heart Monitor layer, add a 100% Opacity keyframe at time 8;15 and a 0% Opacity keyframe at time 9;29.

5   Add the Car Movie composition to the Heartbeat Master Timeline at time 0;00, above the Heart Monitor layer.

6   To fade the Car Movie layer in and out, copy the Heart Monitor layer's Opacity keyframes, paste them onto the Car Movie layer at time 0;00, and then move the third Opacity keyframe to time 5;00 and the fourth keyframe to time 6;00.

Adding Opacity keyframes to fade the layers in and out

7   Set the Car Movie layer's Blending Mode to Add in the Timeline's Modes column. This mode combines the color in the layer with those below it.

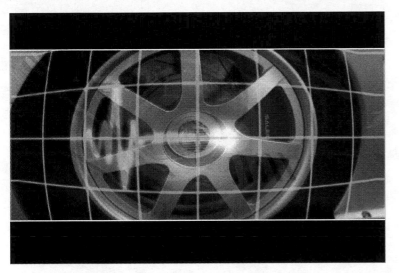

The grid and heartbeat appear within the Car Movie layer.

Now Try This

To add this project's finishing touches, create the following remaining elements:

- To blur the Saleen logo into the scene, drag the **Saleen_logo_Layers** file to the Heartbeat Master Timeline at time 6;00, and duplicate the layer. Move one of the Saleen_logo layers to start at time 7;00. Apply the Fast Blur effect to the Saleen_logo layer that starts at time 6;00.

- Add a letterbox to the scene by adding a new comp-size Solid layer at time 0;00, colored black (RGB: 0, 0, 0). Use the Rectangular Mask tool to outline the letterbox's middle area, and set the Mask Mode to Subtract. Apply Effect > Render > Stroke to the Solid layer to outline the subtracted area with color, and set the effect's Color to white (RGB: 255, 255, 255).

- Add a text layer that displays *THE DRIVE OF YOUR LIFE,* and position it so it appears below the SALEEN logo in the composition window. Fade in this text layer so it appears after the text layer *THE DRIVE...* is totally in focus.

CHAPTER 8 | Exotic Sketch-a-Car

I'm a huge sports car fan, so I was easily inspired when I finally got my hands on a Saleen S7. Taking that car for a spin was an experience right out of the many commercials you've probably seen, where driving appears tantamount to an out-of-body experience as the driver speeds through the countryside. I started thinking about how much fun it must be to design a car like this—not the hard parts, such as aerodynamics, electromechanicals, and such, but drawing the car and watching it come to life. That's when Chapter 8 was born.

In this chapter, you'll use a third-party effect from Boris FX that makes tracing an image of a car like the Saleen S7 quite simple. Not only does the effect create a drawing of the car, but it also automatically animates the drawing as the footage of the rotating car plays. In addition, you'll learn how to make the drawing appear to be drawn onto the screen by using a different effect provided in After Effects.

It Works Like This

Check out the **Ch8FinishedProject.mov** file in this chapter's folder on the book's CD. To achieve those results, you'll do the following:

1. Use the Cartooner effect to create animated sketches from video footage.

2. Create a still image from a frame of your footage.

3. Use the Vector Paint effect to matte the car sketch, and animate the matte so the sketch appears to be drawn onscreen.

4. Quickly create some masks that will frame videos with color strokes.

5. Create a gridded background.

6. Use a quick method to isolate the car from its black background.

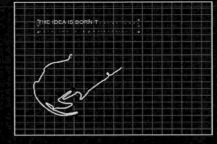

A sketch of the car draws itself onto the screen as the first slogan scales in.

The car reveals itself as other footage plays.

The car footage moves into place as the logo reveals itself.

Preparing to Work

This chapter's project requires four movie clips and a still, all of which are provided on the book's CD. The car sketch you'll design requires the Cartooner effect from Boris FX. To animate the sketch, you'll need the Vector Paint effect, which is only available with the Professional version of After Effects. You'll start by importing the project files and creating a new composition.

To prepare for this project, do the following:

1   This project requires the Vector Paint effect, which is only available with the Professional version of After Effects. If you don't have the Professional version of After Effects installed, you can install a demo version of the software from this book's CD.

2   If you don't have the Continuum Complete collection of effects from Boris FX installed into After Effects, you can install a trial version of the effects from this book's CD. Once you've done so, a slew of submenus named BCC will appear in the Effect menu in After Effects.

3   Start with a new project, and save it as Ch8CarSketch.

4   Import the **Footage** and **Stills** folders from this chapter's folder on the book's CD. The **Footage** folder contains four AVI files: **Saleen_Car_01, Saleen_Car_02, Saleen_Car_4,** and **Saleen_Car_07;** the **Stills** folder contains a PSD file named **Saleen_logo_Layers.**

5   Create a new composition named Car, using the NTSC DV, 720 × 480 composition preset, with Duration 10;00 seconds.

Sketching the Car

There are a number of ways to create a sketch of the Saleen car that is featured in all the movie clips you imported. To make the sketch appear to be drawn onto the screen, you'll animate the Vector Paint effect, so it really doesn't matter how you create the underlying sketch for the initial sequence. You could use one of the filters from the Artistic category in Photoshop to transform the car's appearance into a sketch, or simply draw a stroked path in After Effects. In this project, though, we'll show you how to quickly generate a more malleable sketch by using the Cartooner effect from Boris FX. The primary advantage of using this effect is that the lines the effect generates automatically move as the footage the effect is affecting moves; so, as the Saleen car rotates, the effect's sketch rotates too.

Follow these steps:

1   Place the **Saleen_Car_07.avi** file in the Car Timeline at time 3;00.

2   Apply Effect > BCC3 Effects > BCC Cartooner, and set the effect's property values as listed here:

   Edge Source: None

   Edges From: Luma

   Threshold: 127

   Pre Blur: 2

   Width: Constant

   Stroke Width: 2.5

   Stroke Distance: 0

   Post Blur: 1

   Post Blur Quality: Gaussian Low

   Intensity: 50

   Color: RGB: 235, 235, 235

   Ambient Light, Ambient Follow: 0

   Alpha: Source Alpha

   Reduce Flicker: Off

Apply Mode: Normal

Apply Mix: 100

Mix with Original: 0

Pixel Chooser: Off

In addition to outlining the highlights on the car, the Cartooner effect outlined the shape of the object on the left side of the composition. You don't want that object sketched into the scene, so you'll mask it out next:

1 To exclude the shape on the left, use the Pen tool to draw a mask around the Saleen car.

2 The car rotates in the footage, so go to time 6;00 and adjust the shape of the mask if the mask cuts off the car's shape.

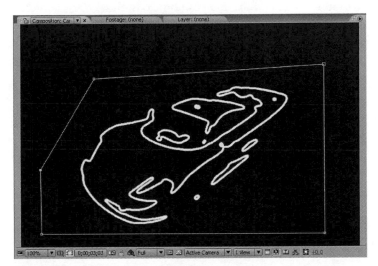

Masking the car to restrict the layer's visible area

Settings for the BCC Cartooner effect in the Effect Controls window

The Cartooner effect applied to the Saleen_Car_07 layer

Capturing a Still

You need the car to stay still as it's sketched onto the screen, but the car in the Saleen_Car_07 layer begins rotating as soon as the footage is played. To get around this behavior, you'll capture the first frame of the footage and add the resulting file to the Car Timeline. The captured Photoshop file will play first, followed by the car's footage. You'll animate the Cartooner effect to create a transition between the two sequences:

1   To capture a frame of the composition, go to time 3;00, choose Composition > Save Frame As > File, and save the file as **Car (0;00;03;00).psd** to the same location as the main project file. (Notice that the default filename helpfully reflects the name of the comp and the current time.)

The Render Queue window opens for you to render the frame to a file in the next step.

2   Expand the Output Module option in the Render Queue window, set the Post-Render Action option to Import, and then click Render.

When the rendering is complete, the rendered frame appears in the Project window using the name that you assigned it.

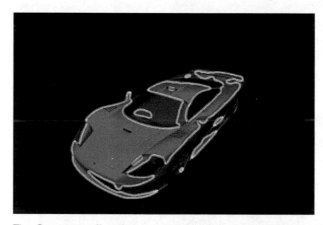

Rendering the captured frame with the Render Queue window

3   Place the **Car (0;00;03;00).psd** file in the Car Timeline so it starts at time 0;00 and is above the Saleen_Car_07 layer.

4   Go to time 3;00, and press Alt (Windows) or Option (Mac OS) and the] key to trim the Car (0;00;03;00) layer's Out point to the current time.

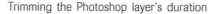

Trimming the Photoshop layer's duration

5   Still at time 3;00, add a Mix With Original keyframe with a value of 0.0 to the Saleen_Car_07 layer's BCC Cartooner effect.

6   Go to time 5;00, and change the Mix With Original value to 100%.

The Cartooner effect fades away to reveal the Saleen car.

Click the Ram Preview button in the Time Controls palette to view the current results. The still of the sketched car plays (actually, it sits still—heh, heh) for the first three seconds, and then the outlines of the car fade away to reveal the car footage.

Animating the Sketch

It's time to animate the car sketch so it appears to be drawn onscreen. Instead of animating the lines in the frame that you captured from the Saleen_Car_07 footage, you'll animate a continuous paint stroke that you'll draw with the Vector Paint effect. The paint stroke will serve as a matte, which you'll animate to reveal the car's sketch over time:

1 Rename the Car (0;00;03;00) layer to AniSketch in the Car composition.

2 Apply Effect > Paint > Vector Paint to the AniSketch layer. Expand the effect's Brush Settings group, and then set the effect's Radius to 7.0. This brush size will make it easy to cover the entire width of the lines you created with the Cartooner effect.

Set the effect's color to something other than white or black so you can make sure you paint over all the white lines in the car sketch and can see your paint strokes over the black background.

Note: Now that you've applied the Vector Paint effect, notice that Vector Paint tools appear in the upper-left corner of the Composition window. The tools appear only when you have the Vector Paint effect selected in either the Timeline or Effect Controls window.

Selection tool
Paint tool
Eraser tool
Paint brush
Air brush
Square brush
Undo button
Eyedropper tool
Color swatch

The Vector Paint effect's tools and properties

3 Using the effect's Paint tool and Paint brush, trace the car line in the AniSketch layer at time 0;00. Don't release your mouse button until you've traced over every line; trace the car body first and then the accents. The resulting car outline will look pretty messy.

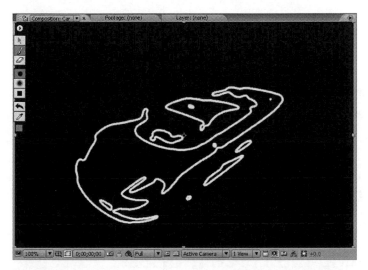

Start the paint stroke where the arrow is pointing in this illustration.

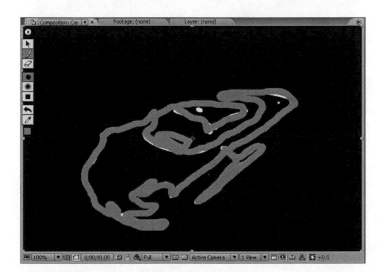

The result of painting over the car lines with the Vector Paint tools

4   Go to time 3;00, and set the Vector Paint effect's Playback Mode to Animate Strokes. When you change the Playback Mode, a new Playback Speed effect property appears, and a short fat stroke appears over only a small part of the car outline.

5   Still at time 3;00, scrub the Playback Speed value until the fat paint stroke completely covers the car outline. You want to find the minimum value that covers the outline completely so there is no delay in the animation when it transitions to the movie layer.

6   Set the Composite Paint option to As Matte. Now you should see the car sketch instead of the Vector Paint stroke.

Click the Ram Preview button in the Time Controls palette to view your animation. The car's sketch should appear to be drawn onscreen by an invisible hand, followed by the footage of the car. If you need to adjust the paint stroke, you must retrace the entire car outline—you can't adjust the stroke as you can other paths in After Effects.

Adding the Three Movies

You've placed, sketched, and animated the primary element of this project: the footage of the Saleen car's exterior. Now you'll stack three smaller videos to the right of the car. After you position and scale the movies, you'll mask them without ever touching the Composition and Timeline windows or the menu commands (intrigued?), and then you'll outline the movies in white to give them more definition.

Here are the steps:

1   To semi-automatically put the remaining footage into the Timeline in the right layer order, click the **Saleen_Car_04.avi** file in the Project window to select it. Then hold down Ctrl (Windows) or Command (Mac OS), and click the **Saleen_Car_02.avi** file followed by the **Saleen_Car_01.avi** file.

2   Go to time 3;00, and drag the selected footage items to the Car Timeline above the other two layers. The new layers should be stacked with the first item you selected in the Project window at the top of the

layer stack, followed by the other items you selected, in the order you selected them. Slide all 3 layers in the timeline so they begin at 3;00.

3   Select the top three layers, press the S key on your keyboard, and set the layers' Scale values to 20, 20%.

4   Reduce the Scale for the AniSketch and Saleen_Car_07 layers to 90, 90%.

5   Set the Position for each layer as follows:

Layer 1: 570, 370

Layer 2: 570, 240

Layer 3: 570, 110

Layer 4: 280, 240

Layer 5: 280, 240

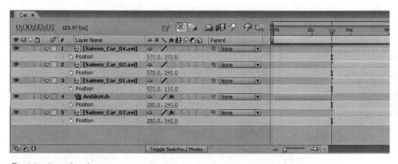

Positioning the layers

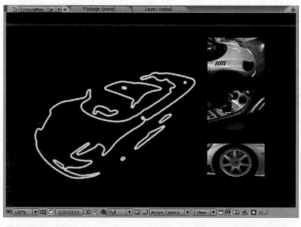

The layout

6 Select the first layer in the Car Timeline, and then double-click the Rectangular Mask tool in the Tools palette to automatically make a mask that surrounds the layer.

Repeat this step for layers 2 and 3.

7 Select all three top layers, and choose Effect > Generate > Stroke. Set the effect's Brush Size property to 15. The effect uses the mask's path by default, so a white line surrounds each video.

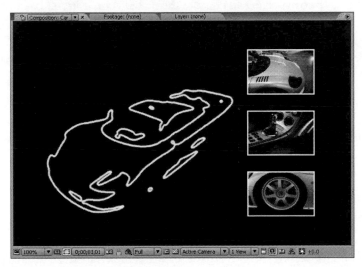

Stroking the three footage items

Sketching the three videos

One of the most useful aspects of the Cartooner effect is that the resulting sketch is automatically animated if the footage you applied the effect to contains motion. For example, if you watch the Saleen_Car_07 layer, you'll see that the lines in the Cartooner effect rotate along with the car the effect sketches. In this section, you'll use the same effect to sketch the three small videos and then fade out the effect to reveal the videos:

1 To keep the three small videos from popping on the screen in unison, move layer 2 to start at time 3;10 and layer 1 to start at time 3;20.

Staggering the In points

2 Go to time 8;00, select the top four layers (not the AniSketch layer), and then press Alt+Shift+T (Windows) or Option+Shift+T (Mac OS) to add a 100% Opacity keyframe to each selected layer.

3 Go to time 9;00, and change the selected layers' Opacity values to 0%.

4 Select only the top three layers in the Car Timeline, and then apply Effect > BCC3 Effects > BCC Cartooner to them.

5 Go to time 4;00, and add a Mix With Original keyframe with a value of 0 to the BCC Cartooner effect for each of the top three layers.

Notice that you must add each keyframe separately; you can't create the keyframe for all three layers simultaneously as you can with native effects.

6 Go to time 5;00, and change the top three layers' Mix With Original values to 100% in the BCC Cartooner effect. This setting fades in the full color of the original movies in unison with the main movie.

Animating the videos

To make room for the logo reveal that closes the animation, you need to animate the three video boxes to slide downward and to the left below the Saleen car:

1   In the Car Timeline, select the top three layers, and press P to display the layers' Position properties.

2   Go to time 6;15, and add Position keyframes to the top three layers.

3   Go to time 7;00, and change the Position values as follows:

>   Layer 1: 170, 370
>
>   Layer 2: 570, 370
>
>   Layer 3: 570, 240

4   Go to time 7;15, and change the Position values as follows:

>   Layer 2: 370, 370
>
>   Layer 3: 570, 370

The final layout of the three video boxes

Adjusting the levels

Now that the base project is complete, you may notice a few things that could use a little adjusting. For starters, the top video box is brighter than the others, and it's a different color. Instead of correcting the top video, though, you'll brighten the other two layers since their tones are a little flat. You'll adjust the color in the next section after you've nested the Car composition into a new parent composition; then you can adjust the color of all the layers by applying an effect to the nested composition.

Follow these steps:

1   Select the Saleen_Car_02 and Saleen_Car_04 layers in the Car Timeline, and apply Effect > Adjust > Levels to the layers.

2   With both layers still selected in the Timeline, set the Levels effect's Input White property to 150 in the Effect Controls window. (Setting this value for one of the layer's Levels effect sets the value for both selected layers.)

Creating a Grid

Now you'll give the project some added pizzazz by creating a gridded background. Creating the grid is easy, thanks to the Grid effect, but making the black area around the Saleen car transparent is tricky. You'll start by creating a new composition to contain the work you've done so far, the grid, and the remaining elements of this project, including the company logo and slogans:

1   Create a new composition named Master, using the NTSC DV, 720 × 480 composition preset, with Duration 10;00 seconds.

2   Drag the Car composition into the Master Timeline starting at time 0;00.

3   Select the Car layer and apply Effect > Color Correction > Hue/ Saturation. Turn on the effect's Colorize option (under the Master Lightness property), and set the effect's Colorize Hue property to 0 x +140.0

4   Go to time 0;00, and create a new comp-size Solid layer named Grid that's any color. (The Grid effect that you'll apply to this layer will override the layer's original color.)

5   Move the Grid layer to the bottom of the layer stack in the Master Timeline.

6   Apply Effect > Generate > Grid to the Grid layer, and set the effect's properties as follows:

> Size From: Width & Height Sliders
>
> Border: 3.0
>
> Opacity: 50.0%
>
> Color: Green (RGB: 0, 255, 0)

7   To fade in the Grid layer, add a 0% Opacity keyframe at time 0;00 and then change the layer's Opacity to 100% at time 0;15.

The underlying grid reveals a black-colored miasma around the car.

Removing the car's black background

The black area that surrounds the car currently covers the underlying areas of the grid and needs to be removed. The first solution that might come to your mind is to use the Color Key effect, which hides all pixels that contain a range of colors that you specify. Unfortunately, the black background contains a wide range of dark hues that also appear within the car; as a result, portions of the car would become transparent, and the grid would appear through the car's frame.

You could use the Inner/Outer Key effect and a new mask drawn around the car to restrict the layer's visibility to the car, but that would require you to animate the mask. That effect provides the best results but requires the most time and patience.

Instead, you'll create a duplicate layer and use blending modes to quickly hide the car's black background:

1   Open the Car composition, and duplicate the Saleen_Car_07 layer.

2   Set the Track Matte of the bottommost Saleen_Car_07 layer to Luma Matte "Saleen_Car_07.avi 2".

3   Add a 100% Opacity keyframe to each Saleen_Car_07 layer at time 6;16, and then change each layer's Opacity to 0% at time 7;15.

Tip: If you return to the Master composition, you'll see that the black area isn't visible around the car; however, the grid bleeds through the car in different areas as a result of the Luma Matte. To fix this, you can add solid layers and mask them to fill in the headlights and windshield; these shapes are simple enough that you can then animate the position of each solid layer as needed.

Adding the Background Car

The background is almost done, now that you've created the grid and fixed up the foreground car. To finish it, you'll add another version of the Saleen_Car_07 footage that you'll make play at a slightly different rate than the original. Do the following:

1 Go to time 3;00 in the Master composition's Timeline, and add **Saleen_Car_07.avi** from the Project window to the Timeline at the bottom of the layer stack.

2 Select the new layer, and choose Layer > Time > Time Stretch. Set the Stretch Factor New Duration to 7;00 in the resulting dialog, and click OK.

   As a result, the layer plays at a slower rate than the same footage that appears in the Car composition.

3 Set the layer's Scale to 200, 200%.

4 Apply Effect > Blur & Sharpen > Fast Blur to the Saleen_Car_07 layer, and set the effect's Blurriness to 10.

5 To fade in the layer, add a 0% Opacity keyframe at time 3;00 and a 100% Opacity keyframe at time 5;00.

6 To fade out the layer, change its Opacity to 50% at time 8;00 and 0% at time 9;00.

Now Try This

To finish your project, you need to add a company slogan that reveals itself as the car is sketched onto the screen and another slogan that replaces the first when the car reveals itself. Both slogans scale themselves into place one character at a time. You can quickly create that effect by using a Text Animator rather than animating the Scale property in the Transform group. In addition, you can animate the Saleen logo for the final closing sequence.

To complete these remaining elements, follow these steps:

1 In the Master composition at time 1;00, add a text layer that displays *THE IDEA IS BORN THAT BECOMES* on one line followed by *EXCELLENCE IN ENGINEERING.*

2 Choose Scale from the layer's Animate menu in the Timeline. Add a Start keyframe and a Scale keyframe to the Animator with a value of 0 for each keyframe, and then change each property's value to 100% at time 3;00.

3 Animate the layer's Opacity from 100% at time 4;00 to 0% at time 5;00.

4 Add the second slogan by duplicating the THE IDEA IS… text layer, and move the top text layer so it starts at time 4;00.

5 Double-click the top text layer in the Timeline to select the characters, and then type AND GIVES BIRTH TO A DREAM on one line and THE INCREDIBLE SALEEN S7 on the next line.

   Because of the Scale and Opacity animation in the text layer, you won't see all the text you type unless you go to time 6;00.

6 Add the **Saleen_logo_Layers.psd** file to the top of the Master Timeline, and then duplicate the layer.

7 Animate the Scale of the bottom logo layer to simulate a text-tracking effect.

8 Apply a Blur effect to the bottom logo layer, and then animate the blur.

9 Animate the Opacity of both logo layers from 0% at time 6;00 to 100% at time 7;00 to fade the layers into the scene.

10 Apply the Drop Shadow effect to the top logo layer.

Tip: To save the text animation (Opacity and Scale) for reuse later in another project, select the text layer in the Timeline, and choose Animation > Save Animation Preset. To save only the Scale animation, expand the text layer's Text group in the Timeline, click the Animator 1 name to select it, and then choose Animation > Save Animation Preset.

CHAPTER 9 | Impact!

by Pete Draper

Blowing Up a Planet

One of the first things many artists do when they start out in 3D is model a planet and blow it up. In this chapter, you will simulate the effect of an object hitting the earth with enough force to generate a nuclear explosion and a shockwave ring that encompasses the earth, showering the planet with debris, scorching and illuminating the surface, and displacing the sea as it passes.

It Works Like This

In this exercise, you will re-create the age-old story of "asteroid meets planet." You will create not only an initial explosion, but also cloud displacement, fiery debris trails, small debris impacts, and a shockwave that scorches the foliage on the planet and displaces the sea. Not a simple task to animate, you might think, and it's not … if you manually keyframe everything. But in this particular example, we have set up the entire scene so that all you have to do is animate a few spinner settings, scale an object or two, and move a few UVW maps.

To lessen the confusion of animating and setting up the entire scene, the scene is divided into several sections. The overall shockwave, cloud displacement, and earth-scorching effects will be material based, so these can be set up as separate tasks and overlaid to generate the final effect. The impact explosion will be material, geometry, and particle based, and the debris impacts will be a simple particle and multiple space warp setup. Finally, you will add a post effect or two to brighten up some elements and to fake impact explosions.

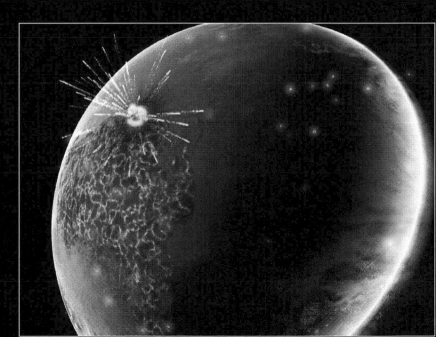

Getting Started

Start with a basic scene, impact.max. The only things you will use that have been previously prepared are several maps to control the effect: a custom Earth Diffuse map (earth diffuse.jpg), a Specular map (earth map reflection.jpg), a Sea map (earth map sea bump mask.jpg), a Burn mask (earth map burn mask.jpg), a Cloud map that comes with max (CloudMap.jpg, located in 3ds max 4's Maps/Space folder), and an Impact Mark mask (impact mark.jpg). These can all be found on the accompanying CD-ROM in this chapter's folder.

An Earth material consisting of the earth diffuse.jpg, earth map reflection.jpg, and CloudMap.jpg images with self-illumination falloff has already been created. This material has been applied to a Nurbs sphere with adaptive detail in the center of the scene and is the subject of a collision with an asteroid (animated for you) that will hit the sphere at frame 200; this gives you a few frames for dramatic build-up! If necessary, you can replace the Nurbs sphere with a sphere geometry primitive. Tesselation is set to Medium by default. Also included in the scene is an Explosion Glow Omni light, created to generate an initial glow blast, with an animated Attenuation and Multiplier. Because none of the lights are set to cast shadows, don't worry about turning off relevant cast/receive shadows in the properties of any of the items in this exercise.

Note: The custom earth bitmaps were created in Photoshop by masking all colors apart from the green foliage for the burn mask. For the sea bump mask, all colors apart from blue were masked out. These custom bitmaps will be used to overlay maps on existing maps assigned to the Earth object to generate the desired effect.

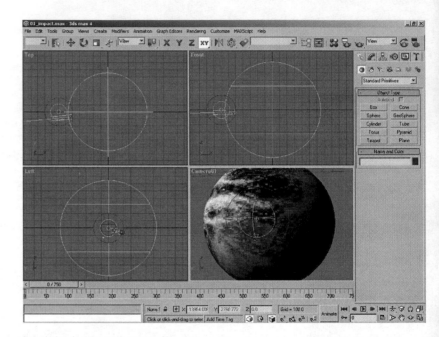

Load the basic max scene file.

Creating the Displaced Clouds Texture

To simulate the initial force of the impact, you will create a cloud displacement/evaporation effect using a gradient opacity that is controlled by a UVW map.

1   Open the Material Editor and click the Earth material in slot one.

2   Navigate to the Diffuse Color, click the Mix Amount slot, and in this Clouds Bitmap map, click the Bitmap button next to the Clouds Bitmap text and add a new Mask map. Check Keep Old Map as Sub-map and click OK. Name this Mask map **Clouds & Nuclear Opacity**.

Using this method, you are creating a new map but are including the existing map as one of its components.

3   Click the Mask slot and add a Gradient Ramp map. Name this **Cloud Displacement Gradient Mask**. Set up the gradient as illustrated.

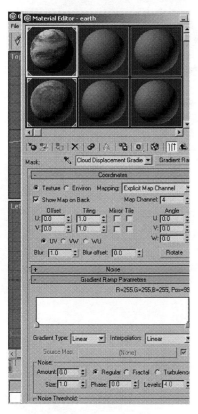

Set up the gradient parameters as shown.

There should be one point at position 99 and one at position 0, both set to white, and the one at position 100 should be set to black.

4   Increase the Map Channel spinner to **4** and turn off U and V tiling. Expand the Output rollout and turn on Invert.

5   Click the Go to Parent button twice to go back to the earth and clouds mix level, and instance copy the Mix slot into the Color #2 slot. This gradient will be used to mask out a section of the cloud layer when the asteroid hits the planet and will be controlled by a UVW map. The gradient is inverted because it is not tiled; any area outside the UVW Map gizmo is normally set to black. Inverting it makes it white, therefore displaying the cloud layer when the UVW gizmo is positioned off the sphere. Inverting the gradient is necessary because you will use it and invert it in another map later on without disturbing any settings.

6   Return to the Earth top-level material and click the Specular Level slot.

You will notice that the Clouds & Nuclear Opacity Mask map is already here. This is because the original material was an instanced copy of the one you previously changed and therefore changed this one also.

7   In this earth minus clouds ref Mix map, add a new Mask map in the Color #2 slot (name this new Mask map **Inverted Clouds**) and keep old map as sub-map. Instance copy the Cloud Displacement Gradient Mask into the Inverted Clouds Mask slot.

The Earth material, by default, has an inverted Cloud map mixed with an Earth Reflection map so that their specular highlights do not smudge together. Therefore, when the cloud is displaced, the Cloud Specular map also needs to be masked out, hence using the same gradient to mask out the same section but on an inverted Cloud map (the Color #2 slot).

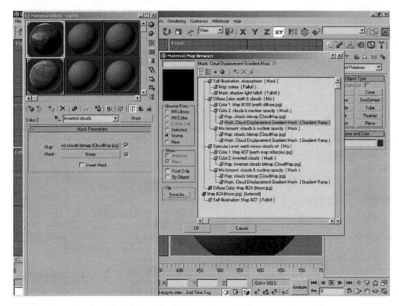

Instance copy the Gradient Mask by selecting Browse From Scene and select the Cloud Displacement Gradient Mask map.

8   Select the Earth Nurbs sphere. Add another UVW Map modifier and set it to Planar with a Map Channel of **4**. Name this **UVW Cloud Displacement**. In the Top viewport, select the modifier's gizmo and move it left along the X-axis so that it is just in front of the sphere.

It is worthwhile to turn on Show Map in Viewport in the Cloud Displacement Gradient Mask Gradient Ramp map to position it correctly.

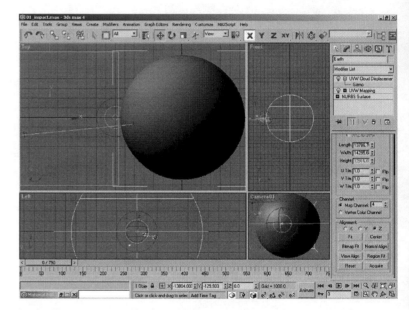

In the Top viewport, create a UVW map as illustrated and offset the gizmo.

9 To check the displacement, position the UVW gizmo so that it intersects the sphere. Activate ActiveShade in the Camera viewport by right-clicking the Camera text and navigate to Views/ActiveShade.

The Camera viewport should now show the cloud layer being masked out by the Gradient Ramp map. Right-click the ActiveShade viewport and select Close in the Quad menu to return to the Camera view. In the Top viewport, move the gizmo back so that it doesn't intersect the sphere. This is the UVW gizmo that controls the gradients and masks you have just set up; it is assigned to control the displacement of the clouds when the asteroid hits the planet. By offsetting the gizmo beyond the sphere, the entirety of the sphere's Cloud map is, as yet, unaffected.

The intersection of the UVW gizmo should result in the cloud layer being displaced.

Creating the Scorched Earth and Displaced Sea Texture

Because you are mainly concentrating on the impact explosion effect, the animation of the asteroid has already been set up, along with its Visibility Track to hide the geometry from the renderer after the impact. Using multiple-layered procedural textures and gradient opacities, you will then set up and animate the scorched earth and sea displacement textures and blend them with the original Earth map.

1 Copy the Earth material you have been working on and name it **Earth Scorched**.

2 In the Diffuse slot, rename this **Earth & Foam & Clouds**. Click the Color #1 slot and add a new Mix map. Keep the old map as a submap. Name this **Earth & Sea Foam**. In the Mix Amount slot, create a Bitmap map and select the earth map sea bump mask.jpg file. Go up one level to the Mix map.

This mask mixes the Earth bitmap with a procedural map that you will use as foamy water.

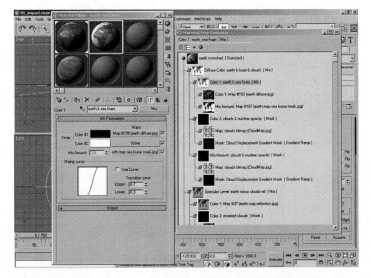

Add the bitmap file to the Mix slot of the new mix material.

3   With the Earth Diffuse bitmap in the Color #1 slot, create a new Mask map in the Color #2 slot. Name this **Waves Overlay**.

4   Create a Noise map in the Mask slot; set it to **Turbulence** with a High of **0.5**. Name this **Wave Foam Mask**.

5   Go up one level to the Waves Overlay Mask map and create a new Gradient Ramp map in the Map slot. Name this **Waves**. Set the Map Channel to **2**, turn off U and V tiling, and create a gradient of waves using a fading white and a dark blue with an RGB of 11, 21, 48 as illustrated.

    This time, the gradient is used as a map and not as a mask, but it will be controlled in the same way as before, with the use of UVW Map gizmos. This gradient is masked out by a procedural Noise map and is mixed in with the earth bitmap only where there is water, using the earth map sea bump mask.jpg bitmap.

6   In the Earth Modifier stack, right-click the UVW Cloud Displacement modifier, copy it, right-click again, and paste. Rename the new UVW Modifier **UVW Transition** and set the Map Channel spinner value to **2**.

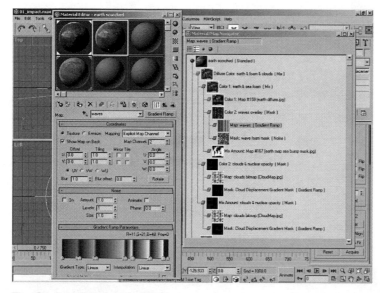

The Gradient Ramp wave design.

This ensures that both maps start their animation in the same place. Now you will create the Scorched Earth texture.

7   At the top level, add a new composite map to the Self-Illumination slot. Keep old map as sub-map. Name this **Atmosphere & Fire**.

8   In the Map 2 slot, add a new Mask map and name it **Scorch**. In the Scorch Mask slot, add the earth map burn mask.jpg bitmap.

9   In the Map slot, add a new Noise map set to **Turbulence** with a Size of **200**, a High of **0.5**, and **10** Levels. Click the Swap button to flip the white and black colors. Name this new Noise map **Fire Noise Patches**.

10 In the Noise Parameters Color #1 slot, add another new Noise map and name it **Red Fire**. Set it to **Turbulence** with a Size of **200**, a High of **0.3**, and **10** Levels. Set the Color #2 for this new Noise map to red (R 255, G 0, B 0).

You can test the Earth Scorched map by assigning it to the Earth sphere.

11 Again, in the Color #1 slot of the Red Fire map, add another Noise map and name it **Yellow & White Fire**. Set it to **Turbulence** with a Size of **200**, a High of **0.2**, and **10** Levels. Set Color #1 to white and Color #2 to yellow (R 255, G 225, B 0).

Note: You have created a multilayered map to generate a fire effect using multiple Noise maps layered on top of each other to generate the required result because the fire effect requires more than two colors and different sizes. This effect has been masked out by the earth map burn mask.jpg bitmap and composited with the atmosphere map in the Self-Illumination slot.

Creating the Impact Mark

Using the gradient opacity created for the displaced clouds, you will now add an impact mark on the earth's texture.

1 In a new material slot, create an Oren-Nayar-Blinn material with Specular Level and Glossiness set to **0**. Name it **Impact Mark**.

2 In the Diffuse slot, create a Gradient Ramp map and name it **Impact Fire**. Set the Map Channel to **3** and turn off U and V tiling. Change the Gradient Type to Radial.

3 Create a gradient like the one illustrated by using colors from white at positions 0 and 5, to yellow (R 255, G 255, B 0) at position 10, to orange (R 255, G 100, B 0) at position 16, to dark red (R 130, G 0, B 0) at position 33, and finally to black at positions 60 and 100. In the Gradient Ramp Parameters, increase the Noise Amount to **0.1**, Fractal, and **0.1** Size.

4 Go up to the top-level material and instance copy the Impact Fire Gradient Ramp into the Self-Illumination slot.

5 In the Opacity slot, create a Mask map and name it **Impact Mark & Mask**. In the Map slot, add a new Bitmap map and add the impact mark.jpg bitmap. Turn off U and V tiling and set the Map Channel spinner to **3**.

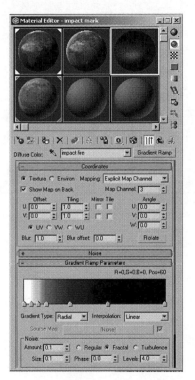

Design the gradient using the settings illustrated.

6 In the Impact Mark & Mask mask slot (the parent map), instance copy the Cloud Displacement Gradient Mask previously created.

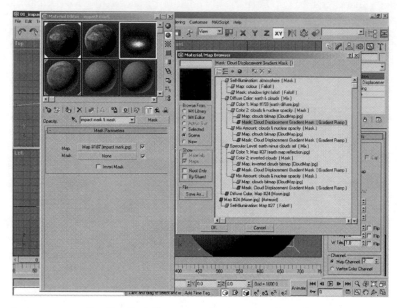

Instance copy the Gradient Ramp map by browsing from the scene.

7 In the Impact Mark & Mask mask map, check Invert Mask.

Inverting the gradient occludes the impact mark until the cloud displacement UVW map intersects the sphere. The inverted gradient is inverted again; because it is not tiled, any area outside the UVW Map gizmo is set to white (normally black, but the gradient is inverted). Hence, you now invert it back to black to occlude the impact mark without affecting the instance.

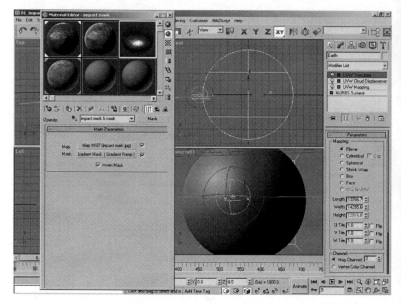

The Mask map's mask is inverted here, not inside the Gradient Ramp map.

8   In the Top viewport, add a new UVW Map modifier to the earth's stack, name it **UVW Impact Mark**, and set the Map Channel spinner to **3**. Select the Gizmo sub-object, select Rotate, and enter **−90** in the Y transformation spinner so that it is facing from inside the sphere out to the impact site.

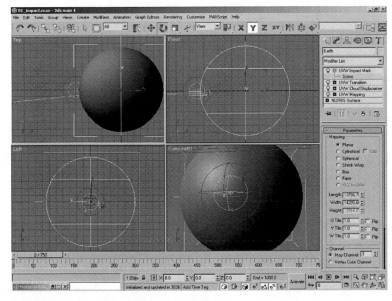

The resulting rotation.

9   Select Uniform Scale and turn on the Absolute Transform Type-In button at the bottom of the screen. Enter **20** in the X entry box.

Scaling the gizmo, not tiling the Impact Opacity map, and using the same map channel and gradient as the Cloud map will properly display the impact mark at the same time as the Cloud layer is masked out.

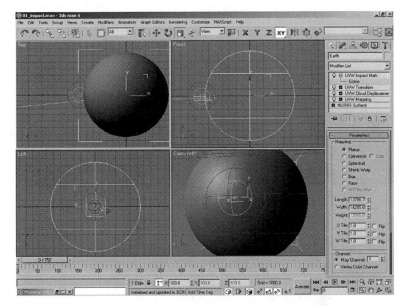

The resulting uniform scale.

Creating the Shockwave

Finally, you will create the shockwave blast that will illuminate the Earth texture in front of and behind its wake.

1   Create a new Oren-Nayar-Blinn material and name it **Shockwave Gradient**. Set the Ambient, Diffuse, and Specular colors to white, set Self-Illumination to **100**, and set Specular Level and Glossiness to **0**.

For an overlay like this (and the impact mark), it is always best to use custom or no specular and glossiness settings because they will also be overlaid.

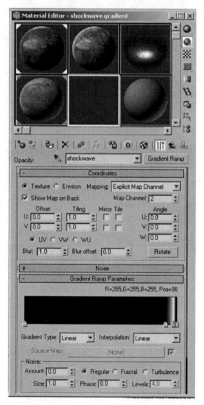

The Shockwave Gradient Ramp map settings.

2   In the Opacity slot, create a new Gradient Ramp map and name it **Shockwave**. Turn off U and V tiling and set the Map Channel spinner to **2**. Design the gradient as illustrated: black at positions 0, 93, 99, and 100 and white at position 98.

This is the band of white that will pass over the sphere, controlled by the same UVW gizmo that controls the cloud displacement and impact mark opacities. You will now get the shockwave to illuminate the earth's surface.

3   In the Earth material, add a new Mix map to the Self-Illumination slot and keep old map as sub-map. Name this **Atmosphere & Shockwave Illumination**.

4   In the Color #2 slot, instance copy the Earth & Clouds Mix map previously created.

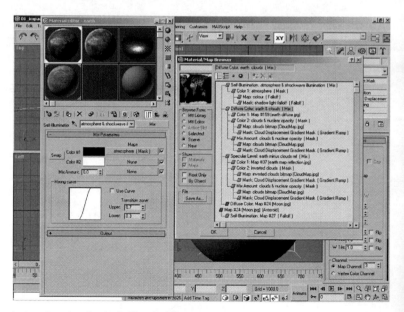

Instancing the Earth & Clouds Mix map.

5   In the Mix Amount slot of the Atmosphere & Shockwave Illumination Mix map, copy (not instance) the Shockwave Gradient Ramp to create a new map. Name this new gradient **Shockwave Glow**.

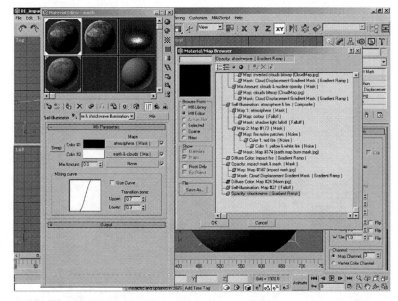

Copy the Shockwave Gradient Ramp map by selecting Browse From Material Editor and selecting the Shockwave Gradient Ramp map.

6   Delete the black flag at position 99 and move the black flag at position 93 to 87.

This enables you to slightly modify the gradient to illuminate the Earth map in front of and behind the Shockwave gradient, with the intensity building up to the front of the shockwave and fading out behind it.

Amend the Gradient Ramp settings to those illustrated.

Putting the Materials Together

By using Blend and composite materials, you will overlay each material to generate one fully animated composite material that will be applied to our Earth object.

1   Create a new Blend material and name it **Earth Blend**. Instance copy the Earth material to the Material 1 slot and the Earth Scorched material to the Material 2 slot by dragging them to the Blend material's slots.

2   Copy the Shockwave Gradient Ramp to the Mask slot. Name the new gradient **Earths Gradient** and amend the gradient flag positions so there are black flags at positions 87 and 100 and white ones at positions 0 and 69.

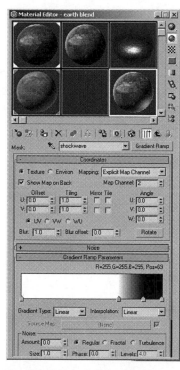

Amend the copied Gradient Ramp to the illustrated settings.

This is the transition gradient from the normal Earth material to the scorched copy. You are using Blend for this material because the composite material you will use to assemble the complete material overlays materials that can produce undesired results such as brightening or additive compositing. This is acceptable for the other materials because they are designed to do so.

3   Create a new composite material and name it **Earth Composite**. Instance copy the Earth Blend material to the Base Material slot, instance the Impact Mark material to the Material 1 slot, and instance the Shockwave Gradient material to the Material 2 slot. Uncheck every other material in the composite material. Assign the composite material to the Earth Nurbs sphere.

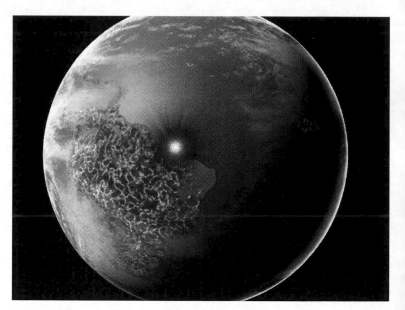

A test render with the composite material applied to the Earth sphere and the UVW gizmos offset. The Impact mark is revealed, the clouds are displaced, and the scorched surface can be viewed.

Animating the Materials

Now that all that hard work has been done, all you need to do now is animate the UVW Cloud Displacement and UVW Transition gizmos.

1 Scrub the time bar across to frame 750 and turn on Animate. Turn on Smooth + Highlights in the Top and Left viewports (if they are not on already), and turn on Show Map in Viewport in the Shockwave Gradient Ramp.

2 In the Top viewport, move the UVW Transition gizmo along the X-axis to the right of the sphere so that it passes over it, roughly up to about 3/4 of the way across.

This animates the position of the shockwave, controls the self-illumination of the planet's surface, and controls the transition from the Earth material to the Scorched Earth material including the sea foam waves.

3 Scrub back to frame 225. Turn on Show Map in Viewport in the Cloud Displacement Gradient Mask Gradient Ramp. Select the UVW Cloud Displacement gizmo and move it slightly to the right in the Top viewport so that it just intersects the sphere.

The resulting map will be just slightly larger than the Moon Nurbs sphere when viewed in the Left viewport.

4 Turn off Animate. In the timeline, drag-select the key(s) at frame 0 and drag them to frame 200.

This offsets the start time of the impact effects to frame 200, when the asteroid intersects the Nurbs sphere.

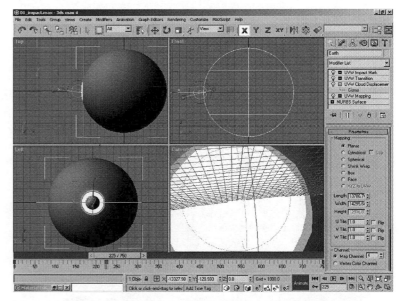

Moving the UVW Cloud Displacement gizmo in the Top viewport while viewing it in the Left viewport.

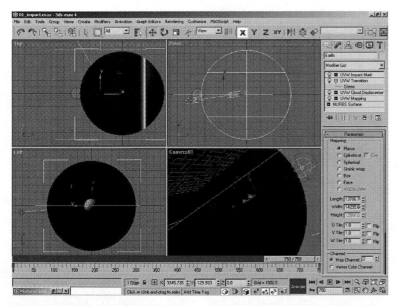

Moving the UVW Transition gizmo across the Nurbs sphere.

Creating the Impact Explosion and Initial Impact Glow

Now that the Earth Impact material is set up, you will add a few pyrotechnics to the scene. The impact fireball will be created using a Scatter compound object with an animated emitter, allowing the fireball to grow. We will then add a subtle glow to the Scatter object to give the impression of intense illumination.

1   Create a geosphere primitive in the Left viewport with a radius of **50** and **3** segments; make it a Tetra Base Type and name it **Explosion Fireball**.

2   Create another geosphere primitive in the Left viewport at X = 0, Y = 0, Z = 0 with a radius of **100** and **10** segments; name this **Scatter Explosion Emitter** and make it a Tetra Base Type. Check Base to Pivot and select Move. Enter **–6500** in the X Transformation Type-In

box at the bottom of the screen so that the geosphere sits just on the surface of the Nurbs sphere.

3   Scrub the timeline to 750 and turn on Animate. Increase the Radius value to **300** and move the radius key generated at frame 0 in the timeline to frame 200. Turn off Animate.

4   Select the Explosion Fireball geosphere and create a Scatter compound object; select the Scatter Explosion Emitter geosphere as the Distribution Object. Increase the amount of duplicates to **100**, check Use Maximum Range and Lock Aspect Ratio in the Scaling section in the Transforms rollout, and enter a value of **100** in the X percentage spinner. Check Hide Distribution Object in the Display rollout.

5   Select the Explosion Fireball Scatter object and the Scatter Explosion Emitter and open Track View. Add a Visibility Track to both the Scatter Explosion Emitter and the Explosion Fireball. Create keys in the visibility track of the Scatter Explosion Emitter at frames 199 and 200 with values of **0** and **1**, respectively.

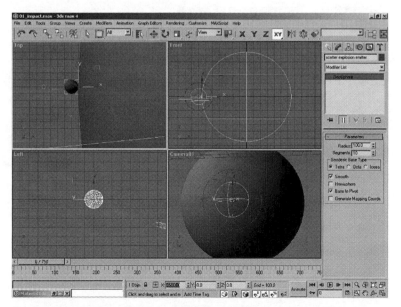

Create the geosphere in the Left viewport and move it by entering the transformation value in the X Transformation Type-In box.

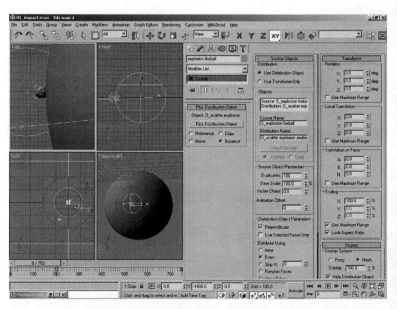

Create the Scatter compound object with these settings.

6 Select the Visibility Track with the created keys and click the Copy icon in Track View. Select the Visibility Track for the Explosion Fireball and instance paste by clicking the Paste icon in Track View.

Because you do not want to see the explosion before frame 200 (when the asteroid hits), using Visibility Tracks enables you to hide the Scatter and Emitter objects before frame 200 and then display them on and after frame 200.

7 Create a new Blinn material and name it **Explosion Fireball**. Give it a Material ID of **1**, check 2-Sided, and set Specular and Glossiness to **0**. Check the Color box in the Self-Illumination box and leave the color as black.

8 Create a Towards/Away Falloff map in the Diffuse slot; name this **Fire Falloff**. Swap the black and white colors. In the Towards (top) slot, add a Noise map and name this **Fire Noise**. Use Turbulence with a Size of **200**, a High of **0.75**, and **10** Levels. Click the Swap button.

9 Add another Noise map in the Fire Noise Color #1 slot and name this **Red Fireball Fire**. Give the Color #2 slot value of R 255, G 0, B 0. Change the noise type to **Turbulence** with a Size of **200**, a High of **0.3**, and **10** Levels.

10 Add another Noise map in the Red Fireball Fire Color #1 slot and name this **White & Yellow Fireball Fire**. Make the Color #1 slot white and the Color #2 slot R 255, G 225, B 0. Change the noise type to **Turbulence** with a Size of **200**, a High of **0.2**, and **10** Levels.

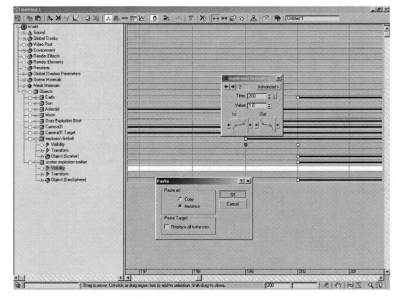

Instance-copying the Visibility Track.

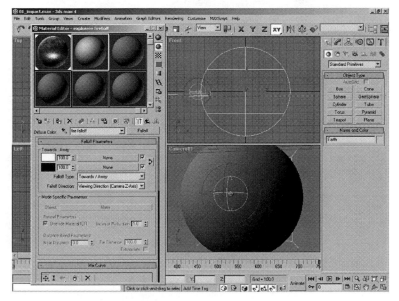

The Towards/Away Falloff map.

11 Back at the top level of the material, instance copy the Fire Falloff map to the Self-Illumination and Opacity slots. In Extended Parameters, change the Advanced Transparency Type to Additive. Assign this material to the Explosion Fireball Scatter object.

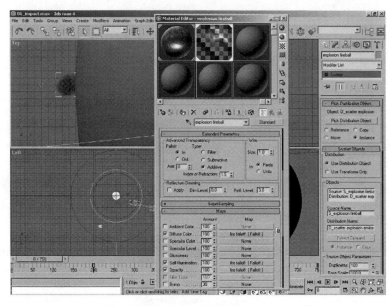

Instance copy the Fire Falloff into the Self-Illumination and Opacity slots and amend the Advanced Transparency settings.

12 Copy the material and name the new one **Explosion Emitter**. Uncheck the Opacity Map. Change the Advanced Transparency Type back to Filter, change the Falloff to Out, and increase the Amount spinner to **100**. Uncheck 2-Sided. Assign this material to the Scatter Explosion Emitter geosphere.

13 In the Rendering Effects window, add a Lens Effects effect and name it **Lens Effects Explosion**. Add a Glow Element to the right pane of the Lens Effects Parameters. Click the new Glow Element.

14 In the Glow Element's rollout, amend the Size spinner to **0.02**. The Intensity, Occlusion, and Use Source Color spinners should each be set to **100**. Turn off Glow Behind.

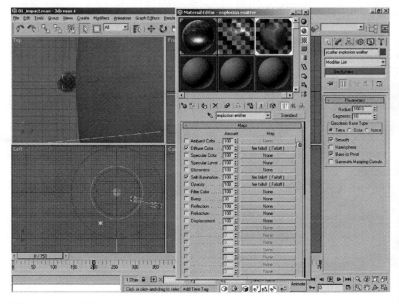

The amended Material settings.

15 In the Glow Element's Options tab, turn off Lights and turn on Effects ID. Make sure the Effects ID spinner is set to **1**.

Because the explosion effect uses additive transparency on the Scatter object, the glow effect need not be too intense as there is already an initial glow. The glow breaks up any harsh edges and adds a sense of intense illumination in the scene.

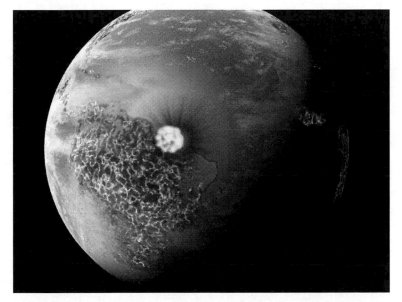

The resulting Scatter object combined with the Scatter emitter at frame 750.

Creating the Impact Fire Debris

To add emphasis to the dramatic scene, you will now add large fiery debris trails emanating from the impact site using additive materials and Particle Spawn.

1 In the Top viewport, at X = −6500, Y = 0, Z = 0, create a Super Spray particle system and name it **Fire Trails**. Rotate it −90 along the Y-axis so that it is facing back out, away from the earth.

2 Give an Off Axis Spread of **100** degrees and an Off Plane Spread of **90** degrees. By default, the Viewport Display type should be set to Ticks. Set Percentage of Particles to view to **5%**.

3 In the Particle Generation rollout, click Use Total and change the spinner value to a value between 10 and 60. Set Particle Motion Speed to **8** and Variation to **30%**.

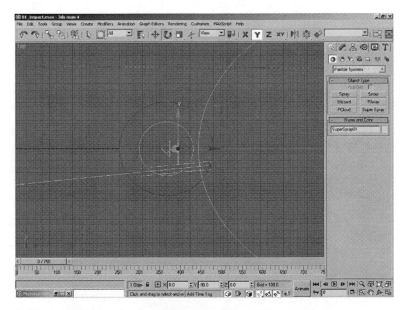

Create and position the Super Spray particle system.

Note: Vary your setting from 10 to 60 in the Use Total spinner; if your computer is not very powerful, you might want to drop the setting down further because a lot of particles will be created later on using Particle Spawn, which will dramatically increase render times. The more particles, however, the better the impact effect.

4   Change the Particle Timing Emit Start and Emit Stop spinners to **200** and the Display Until and Life spinners to **1000**.

5   In the Particle Size section, change the Size spinner to **15** with **50%** Variation. Set the Grow and Fade For spinners to **0**. In the Particle Type Rollout, use Standard Particles set to Facing.

6   In the Particle Spawn Rollout, toggle on Spawn Trails. Change the Direction Chaos spinner to **1%**, the Speed Chaos Factor spinner to **100%**, and toggle on Both. Turn on Inherit Parent Velocity. In the Lifespan Value Queue, enter **500** in the Lifespan spinner and click the Add button.

This is the lifespan for the spawned particle trails, not the emitter particles.

7   Create a new Blinn material and name it **Fire Trails**. Turn on 2-sided and Face Map in the Basic Parameters rollout. Amend the Specular Level and Glossiness spinners to **0** and increase the Self-Illumination spinner to **100**.

8   Under the Extended Parameters rollout, change the Advanced Transparency Type to Additive.

Using additive transparency means you don't have to create a glow effect for the particles.

9   In the Diffuse slot, add a Particle Age map and name it **Trails**. Make Color #3 black and set the Age #2 spinner to **5**. Add a Noise map in the Color #1 slot. Name this **Yellow & Orange**. Set the Low to **0.25**. Set Color #1 to R 255, G 255, B 0 and Color #2 to R 255, G 148, B 0.

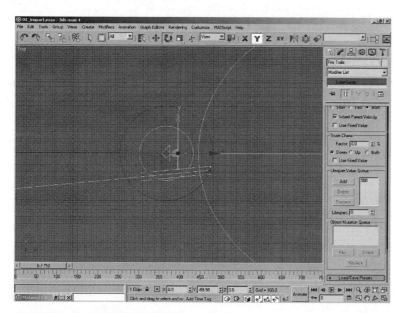

Amend the Super Spray settings to those illustrated.

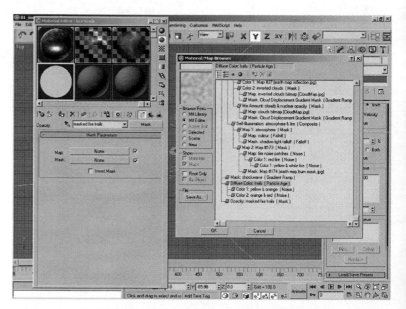

Selecting the Particle Age map to instance into the Map slot.

10 Go up one level to the Trails map, copy the Yellow & Orange Noise map to the Particle Age's Color #2 slot, and name the new map **Orange & Red**. Amend this Noise map's Color #1 slot to R 255, G 148, B 0 and Color #2 to R 255, G 0, B 0.

11 Back at the top, create a Mask map in the Opacity slot and name it **Masked Fire Trails.** Instance copy the Trails Particle Age to the Map slot.

12 Go up one level to the Masked Fire Trails map, add a Gradient map to the Mask slot, and name it **Gradient Circular Mask**. Change the Gradient Type to Radial. Assign the material to the Fire Trails particle system.

Using a Particle Age map enables you to design exactly how you would like the particle colors to change over a particle's life. Using it in conjunction with the circular gradient also enables you to control its density over its life.

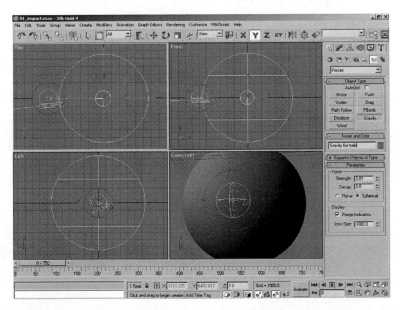

Creating the Gravity Fire Trails space warp.

13 Create a Gravity space warp set to Spherical Force at X = 0, Y = 0, Z = 0. Set the Strength spinner to **0.01**. Name it **Gravity Fire Trails**.

14 Create a SOmniFlect space warp at X = 0, Y = 0, Z = 0 with a radius of **6470** and name it **SOmniFlect Fire Trails**. Under Parameters, increase the Time Off spinner to **750** and set the Reflection Bounce to **0** and Friction to **5**.

15 Bind the Fire Trails particle system to the Gravity Fire Trails and SOmniFlect Fire Trails space warps.

The Gravity space warp pulls the particles back down to the Earth sphere, but the SOmniFlect space warp prevents them from intersecting the sphere, enabling them to skid across the atmosphere.

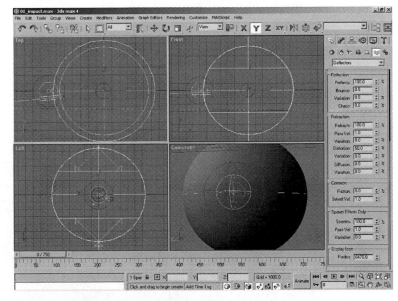

Create the SOmniFlect space warp with the illustrated settings.

Creating the Impact Small Debris Shower

You will now create the small shower of debris that has been kicked up by the blast and is re-entering the Earth's atmosphere and impacting with the surface, using a Super Spray particle system, two space warps, and two low poly instanced spheres with different materials. You will also add an additional impact effect using the Glow effect to slightly illuminate the Earth's surface.

1 Create two sphere primitives, one named **Small Debris Instance** with a Radius of **10** and **4** segments and the other named **Small Debris Impact** with a Radius of **40** and **6** segments.

2 In the Top viewport, create another Super Spray particle system at X = –7000, Y = 0, Z = 0. Name it **Small Debris**. Rotate it –90 along the Y-axis so that it is facing back out, away from the earth.

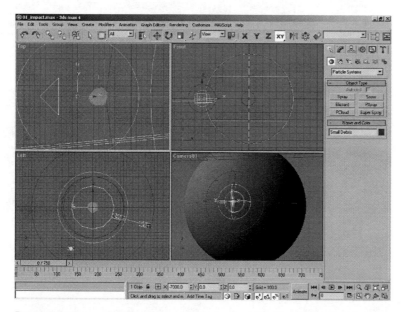

Position the new particle system just in front of the Fire Trails particle system.

3 Set the Off Axis Spread and the Off Plane Spread spinners both to **90** degrees. Amend the Percentage of Particles spinner to **5%**.

4 Under the Particle Generation rollout, increase the Use Rate spinner to **300**. Set the Particle Motion Speed spinner to **100** and the Variation spinner to **50%**. Set the Particle timing Emit Start and Stop spinners to **200** and the Display Until and Life spinners to **1000**. Set the Grow For and Fade For spinners to **0**.

5 Under the Particle Type rollout, change the Particle Types to Instanced Geometry, click the Pick Object button under Instancing Parameters, and select the Small Debris Instance sphere.

6 Under the Particle Spawn rollout, check Spawn on Collision. Add **1000** to the Lifespan Value Queue. Under the Object Mutation Queue section, click the Pick button and select the Small Debris Impact sphere.

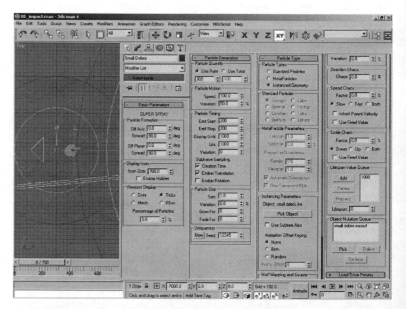

Amend the particle system's settings to those illustrated.

7 Create a new Blinn material and set the Glossiness and Opacity to **0**. Name this **Small Debris Instance** and assign it to the Small Debris Instance sphere.

Note: Due to the way Particle Spawn works, particles can only change their color with spawn on collision if Instanced Geometry is the main particle type. Therefore, you will use a transparent material for the main particles to hide them from the scene and another material and object for the spawned particles. At a later date, you might want to see the initial particles emit from the explosion, in which case you can amend the Small Debris Instance material properties.

---

8 Copy the Explosion Fireball material, rename the copy **Small Debris Impact Explosion,** and amend its Material ID from 1 to **2**. Assign this to the Small Debris Impact sphere. Hide the Small Debris Instance and Small Debris Impact spheres.

9 In the Small Debris particle system, click the Get Material From button in the Mat'l Mapping and Source section of the Particle Type rollout.

10 Copy the Gravity Fire Trails space warp and name the new space warp **Gravity Small Debris**. Amend the Strength spinner to **0.5**.

11 Create a SOmniFlect space warp at X = 0, Y = 0, Z = 0 with a Radius of **6470** and name it **SOmniFlect Small Debris**. Under Parameters, increase the Time Off spinner to **750**, set the Reflection Bounce to **0**, and Friction to **100**.

12 Bind the Small Debris particle system to the Gravity Small Debris and SOmniFlect Small Debris space warps.

By using Particle Spawn, the initial particles are pulled back to the Earth sphere and are replaced with the larger self-illuminating particles when they hit the SOmniFlect Small Debris space warp, which holds them in place due to the high Friction value.

13 In the Rendering Effects window, add a Lens Effects effect and name it **Lens Effects Small Debris Impacts**. Add a Glow Element to the right pane of the Lens Effects Parameters. Click the new Glow Element.

14 In the Glow Element's rollout, amend the Size spinner to **0.1**, Intensity to **120**, and the Occlusion and Use Source Color spinners to **100**. Turn off Glow Behind. In the Glow Element's Options tab, turn off Lights, turn on Effects ID, and set the Spinner to **2**.

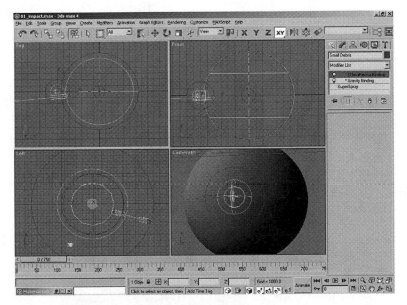

The resulting particle systems' modifier stack.

Final Animation

Now it is time to put the entire scene together. It will become apparent why an additional UVW map for the Earth map and the Cloud Layer map was included, even if you used a sphere primitive with Generate Mapping turned on. You can simply rotate the Spherical UVW map so that the asteroid hits any place on the planet without disturbing or having to amend the position of the other UVW maps and the other elements of the scene.

1   Pick a continent that has a large amount of green in it (such as the Americas, Europe, or Asia) and target the impact on the continent's coastline to view both the sea's wave and the scorched earth effect at frame 200. Scrub the time bar back to frame 0.

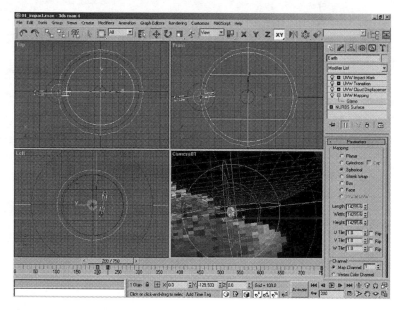

Amend the UVW Mapping modifier's gizmo to rotate the Earth texture map without affecting the other maps you have set up.

2   Go to Video Post, add a Camera event and a Starfield Image filter event (with the Scene camera as the selected camera, about 30,000 stars, and the default Motion Blur settings), and add an Image Output event. Render the animation.

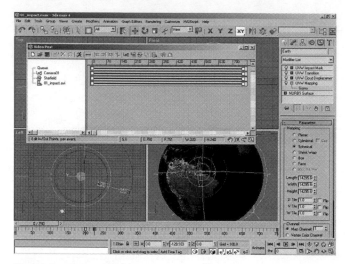

The Video Post sequence.

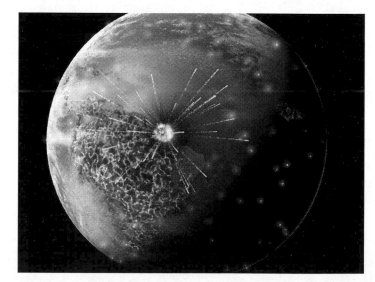

The final animation at frame 500.

Modifications

There are, of course, any number of enhancements you could make to this scene. Additional elements could be added, such as binding the large debris particle trails to the Earth object deflector and increasing the gravity on the particle system's Gravity space warp. This will then pull the trails closer to the earth and, upon impact, remain stationary until they die. This gives a very nice effect, although it is a very CPU-intensive operation. Also, you could add different starfield backgrounds and other galactic phenomenon such as the Milky Way or nebulae.

You could also change the asteroid to a comet or even multiple smaller meteors using particles and generate impacts as illustrated in this chapter. You could add elements of civilization, such as satellites, space junk, and pinpoint lights, to represent cities on the dark side of the planet. There are numerous plug-ins that could enhance your scene, namely Cebas Pro Optics Suite, Ultrashock, Outburst, Phoenix, or Afterburn; there are also a few freeware ones around, such as FreePyro.

The overall effect mainly depends on which disaster movie you are basing your animation on! For this particular one, I mainly concentrated on the blockbuster *Armageddon*, but you might not altogether agree with the global (pardon the pun) effect of the impact. Look at other disaster movies such as *Deep Impact*, *Mission to Mars* (although the Mars impact is rather short), and *Dinosaur*, and you will get a different artist's representation of pretty much the same event. You could also incorporate additional cut scenes such as the asteroid entering the atmosphere and passing through a cloud layer (displacing clouds) and another for the sea or land impact before cutting back to outer space.

CHAPTER 10 | Camera Matching

by Marcus Richardson

Realistically Insert a 3D Model into a Piece of Digital Video

In today's industry of special-effects-loaded movies and the pursuit of lifelike computer graphics, you would be hard pressed to find a movie that does not have some sort of 3D aspect to it. Taking a piece of video and successfully inserting 3D characters and models into it is what has made movies like *Star Wars: Episode I, The Matrix,* and *X-Men* the brilliant visual-effect masterpieces that they are. 3ds max 4 has the tools to give you the power of a multimillion-dollar effects studio. In this tutorial, you will learn how to use a section of digitally shot video, simple geometry, and lighting to create an environment for your 3D models and animations to exist in. You will see how easy 3ds max 4 makes it for you to create your own professional-looking animations and video!

It Works Like This

In this exercise, you will be using a simple probe droid–looking model. This will enable you to concentrate more on the lighting, camera angles, and reflections rather than having to worry about complex animation. Keep in mind, though, that after you have set up the scene properly, you will be able to import your own models and animation into the scene. This particular exercise will be using still video to get you used to max's tools. Using moving video requires precise measurements, led tracking points, and a lot of extra steps that would make it impossible to teach in one tutorial. As the background for the scene, you will be using a digital video segment of a dark, rainy alley shot on a tripod to reduce camera movement. Its resolution is 720×480, which is standard for digital video. This means that after you are done with this tutorial and have put your own characters into the scene, you can put it on video-tape and marvel with your friends at how cool you are!

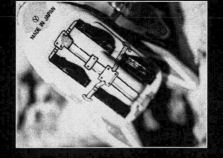

"If you want to be successful in a particular field of endeavor, I think perseverance is one of the key qualities. I haven't met anyone (who is successful) who hasn't been able to describe years and years of very, very difficult struggle through the whole process of achieving anything whatsoever. There's no way to get around that."

—GEORGE LUCAS

Getting Started

To get started, load **CameraMatch01.max** from this chapter's folder on the accompanying CD-ROM. You will see the probe droid and nothing else in the scene. (We have added arms and a simple bone structure to enable you to animate it later.) The droid was made out of a simple sphere, extruding polygons out of it and mapping it with the Space Metal material in the 3ds max 4 Space Material library. You can view the complete file by opening **CameraMatch02.max**.

Setting Up the Camera

This is the meat of this tutorial. You will be creating a free camera and inserting the background.avi. The first thing you need to do is group and hide the droid to get it out of the way.

1   In the Front viewport, drag and select all of the droid. In the top toolbar, click Group and group the droid. Name it **Droid**. Click the Display icon in the right toolbar and click Hide Selected.

    You will unhide the droid later for the animation.

2   Click in the Front viewport to make it active. In the object creation toolbar to the right, click the Camera icon and create a free camera in the Front viewport. You can set its position to X = 0, Y = 0, Z = 0 if you want, but it does not matter because you will be moving the camera anyway.

3   Right-click in the Perspective viewport and press "C" on the keyboard.

    This will set the viewport to the view of the camera you just created.

Note: Another way to select the droid is to click the Select by Name arrow in the top toolbar and click All.

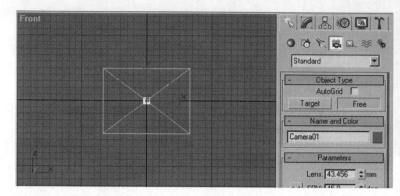

Create a free camera in the Front viewport and use the default settings.

4   Now you need to insert the background AVI into the environment background. In the top menu, click Rendering and navigate down to Environment. Under Common Parameters in the environment pop-up box, click the None button under Environment Map.

This will open the Material/Map Browser.

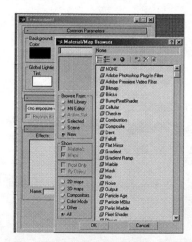

Click the None button to open the Material/Map Browser.

The Material/Map Browser will enable you to insert the background video.

5 Double-click Bitmap. Select **background.avi** from this chapter's folder on the accompanying CD-ROM. Click Open and, after it loads, close out of the Environment settings.

Now you need to get the background.avi to show up in the viewport.

6 At the top of the screen, select Views and select Viewport Background. Under Background Source, click Use Environment Background. At the bottom of the menu, click Display Background and then click OK.

You will see the movie clip appear in the Camera viewport. You need to set the animation length to that of the footage.

Select background.avi from this project's folder on the accompanying CD-ROM.

7 Select File at the top of the screen, and then select View Image File. In the View File dialog, select background.avi from the accompanying CD-ROM and click the Info button.

You will see the statistics of the video clip. It says 720×480, Undefined, 129 frames. You might also notice that there is a bit of blurred video after that.

8 In the Animation Control area at the bottom right of the screen, click the Time Configuration icon. Under the Animation heading, set the Length to **120** to coincide with the number of frames in the movie clip and to edit out the blurred video.

Creating the Ground Plane

Before you continue, I would like to reiterate that you are not using exact measurements. So from here on out, a lot of the work you do will be based on test screen renders and visual interpretation. I prefer this method because it is faster and yields the same results. You will also be typing specific coordinate sets into the new Absolute Transform Type-In boxes at the bottom of the screen. First, however, you need to make sure to set up your units correctly.

1 Click Customize at the top of the screen and then Units Setup. Click US Standard and select Feet w/Decimal Inches.

I stepped off this alley from the camera to the end, and it measured roughly 100 yards. There are 3 feet in a yard, so in the Top viewport, you need to create a box that is 300 feet long.

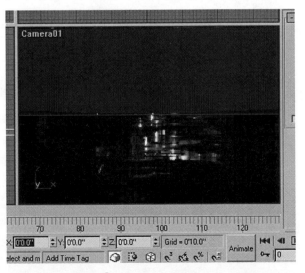

Camera view of the Ground plane when created.

2   Type in the dimensions of **300'0.0"×1'0.0"**. Name the plane **Ground**.

Now you will be visually adjusting the camera to place the Ground plane in the proper position.

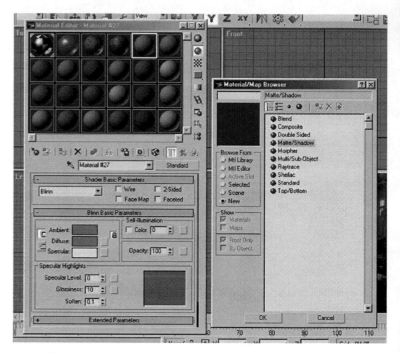

The new Absolute Transform Type-In boxes
at the bottom of the screen.

Note: If you created the plane at X=0, Y=0, Z=0 world coordinates, you'd see the box being clipped by the camera. This is okay because you will be moving the camera.

---

3   In the Top viewport, select the camera, click the Move tool, and type in the transform coordinates of X = −19'6.0", Y = −248'0.0", Z = 83'0.0".

You will see that the box no longer is being clipped, but it is still at the wrong angle.

4   To adjust the plane angle, you need to rotate the camera. With the camera still selected, click the Rotate tool and type in the rotation coordinates of X = 84.5, Y = −0.017, Z = −0.017.

Now you will notice that the angle is starting to look correct, but the ground is still too short. Like I said, you don't have exact measurements.

5   Select the Ground box and type in the Length **4200'0.0"**. You will now apply a Matte/Shadow material to the object.

Note: You can change between Wireframe mode and Shaded mode by pressing the F3 key. This will become very handy when you start adding more objects to the scene.

---

6   Press "M" on the keyboard. This will open the Material Editor dialog. Select one of the empty spheres. Click Standard/Matte/Shadow. This will open the Matte/Shadow dialog. Make sure you click Receive Shadows. Apply the Matte/Shadow material to the Ground object. You will now do a quick test render to see what you have done.

7   Select the Camera viewport and click the Quick Render Teapot in the Top-sliding menu. See what happened? Nothing! Don't panic, that is exactly what you wanted to do. Create a sphere in the Front viewport and move it down, touching the Ground plane.

Select the Matte/Shadow material.

8 Press the Quick Render button again or your hotkey. You can see that the sphere still looks out of place, but it is resting on the ground.

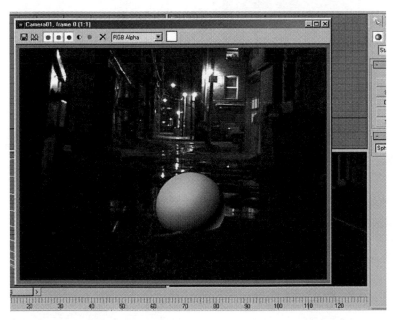

A quick render of the sphere.

Setting Up the Basic Scene Lighting

Okay, now that you have some geometry in the scene, you need to set up the lighting. This step is, I feel, the most important in any camera-matching scenario. Getting the correct lighting is the key to making your objects look like they are part of the scene.

1 Take the sphere you just made and, in the Top viewport, move it back along the Z-axis until it looks like it is in the area of the light shining into the alley. Use X = 0'6.0", Y = 988'0.0", Z = 53'0.0". Go to the Create panel, select the Lights tab, and select Omni.

You are now going to set up a three-point lighting system with omni lights. I have found that this is a great way to give the objects a realistic look.

2 In the Top viewport, create an omni at X = –800'0.0", Y = 0, Z = 0. Make sure Cast Shadows is not checked! Name this light **Backfill**. Click the light you just created, hold down the Shift key, and drag the light to the right. When the Clone dialog appears, select Instance.

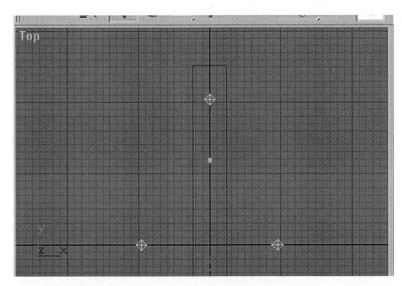

How to arrange the omni lights in the Top view.

This should clone the omni. This is important because it will enable you to adjust all the lights at the same time. You can use the coordinates X = 800'0.0", Y = 0.0", Z = 813'0.0" and name it **Sidefill**.

3   Select the new light, again hold down the Shift key, but this time drag back along the Y-axis. Again, click on Instance. Use X = 3'10.0", Y = 1700'0.0", Z = 1500'0.0". It should already be named Sidefill02. The lights should form a triangle.

4   Go to the Create panel, click Lights/Target Spot, and check Cast Shadows. In the Top viewport, start at the left of the screen and drag the target to the sphere. You can use X = –670'0.0", Y = 1243'10.0", Z = 1168'00.00" for the light and X = 200'0.0", Y = 1200'0.0", Z = 0'0"0.0 for the target. Select the Camera viewport and press your Quick Render key.

You'll notice that you have some depth to the sphere now with a shadow being cast on the ground plane. However, the light is much too bright for this scene.

Note: Because you instanced the omni lights, all of their values are adjusted to 100.

---

5   Click one of the omni lights, adjust the V value of it to **140**, and press your Quick Render key again.

Notice how the sphere looks more like the scene.

6   Click the Spot Light, set its V value to **150**, and Quick Render again.

Note: You might not see a shadow yet, which is fine. You might need to adjust the value of the lights yourself to get the best look for your monitor.

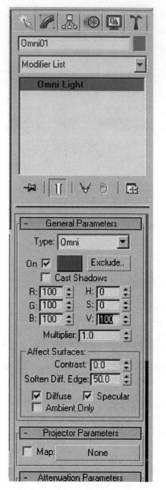

Set the omni light V value to 140.

Creating Scene Objects

Now that you have your lighting set up, you can create masking geometry for objects like the dumpster, the telephone pole, and walls. Before you start, I would like to restate that because we do not have exact scene measurements, a lot of this will be done by eye. I will give you exact sizes and coordinates for this tutorial, but when you try your own pictures and video, you'll have to eye it. It really is not that hard, so stick with it.

1   In the Top viewport, create a box with the dimensions of Length 96'0.0", Width 145'0.0", and Height 200'0.0". Make sure to check Generate Mapping Coordinates and name it **Dumpster1**. Move the box to X = −295'0.0", Y = 390'0.0", Z = −5'0.0". Then select the Rotate tool and rotate the dumpster to X = −2.093, Y = 7.388, Z = −3.27. In the Camera viewport, your scene should look like this.

Note: When doing this on your own, you might find it handy to toggle between Shaded mode and Wireframe mode by using the F3 key. When lining objects up yourself, make the object sizes relative to the scene and then move them around so that the edges match up with the objects in the scene like the dumpster!

The Camera view of Dumpster1.

2   Press the "M" key to bring up the Material/Map Browser and apply the Matte/Shadow material to Dumpster1. Select the sphere and move it to X = −220'0.0", Y = 470'0.0", Z = 53'0.0" in the Top viewport. It should be just partially behind the Dumpster1 object. Press your Quick Render key. You can now start to see how the object masking works.

You can see the sphere behind the dumpster.

Note: Sometimes you will find that the objects do not match up just right, and you get some double imaging. Just move the dumpster and keep pressing Quick Render to get it adjusted correctly. On more complex objects with a lot of sharp, angled edges or round surfaces, you will have to adjust the masking geometry in its Sub-object mode to align it with the movie clip.

---

3 In the Top viewport, create a cylinder with the dimensions of Radius 30'0.0", Height 570'0.0". Name it **Phone pole 2**. Then, still in the Top viewport, place it at X = −287'11.0", Y = 1058'11.0", Z = −11'10.0". Apply the Matte/Shadow material to it. Then move your test sphere to X = −328'0.0", Y = 2100'0.0", Z = 180'0.0". Select the Camera viewport and press your Quick Render key.

Now the sphere appears behind the telephone pole!

4 In the Top viewport, create a cylinder with the dimensions of Radius 8'0.0", Height 570'0.0". Name it **Phone pole 1**. Then, still in the Top viewport, place it at X = 164'2, Y = 1706'7, Z = −3, assuming you want the pole with the light on it. Apply the Matte/Shadow material to it as with the dumpster. Move your test sphere to X = 152'0.0", Y = 2100'0.0", Z = 180'0.0". Select the Camera viewport and press your Quick Render key.

Now the sphere appears behind the other telephone pole.

The sphere appears behind the pole.

5 Create a box in the Top viewport with Length as 80'0.0", Width as 145'0.0", and Height as 474'0.0" and name it **Alleywall**. Place it at X = −456'0.0", Y = 1035'0.0", Z = −5'0.0". Apply the Matte/Shadow material to it. Move your test sphere to X = −430'0.0", Y = 1300'0.0", Z = 97'0.0".

6 Select the Camera viewport and press your Quick Render key. Now the sphere appears behind the alley wall! Select the test sphere and delete it; you do not need it anymore.

Note: You can see now how easy this is! If you wanted to, you could reconstruct all the elements in the screen. But you are not going to because that will not be necessary for your animation.

Animating the Droid

Now you are going to animate the Droid object flying around in the scene. You can follow the animation, or you can make him do whatever you want. Keep in mind that if you make him go behind something that hasn't been created yet, you will have to create those elements on your own using the preceding steps.

1 Under the Create panel, click Display/Unhide By Name. This will bring up the Unhide dialog.

2 Select the Droid Group and click OK. Select the droid, go up to Group at the top of the screen, and click Ungroup. The arms and bones are linked to the main body sphere, so that is the only thing you need to animate.

Note: It is very, very important that, before animating the droid, you ungroup it. If it is not ungrouped prior to animation, the droid's arms will move off its body!

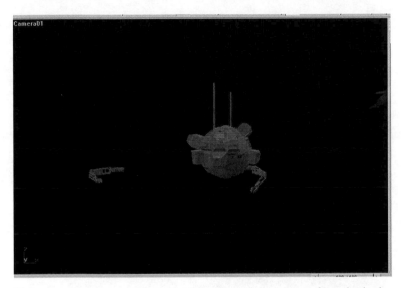

Make sure to ungroup; otherwise, the arms will move away from the body.

3   Click the Droid body sphere and move it to X = 100'0.0",
Y = 2400'0.0", Z = 14'0.0" at the far end of the alley behind the wall.
Turn on the Animate button and move the slider to frame 30. In the
Top viewport, move the droid to X = −90'0.0", Y = 2130'0.0",
Z = 70'0.0".

4   Move the slider to frame 60 and move the droid to X = 170'0.0",
Y = 2080'0.0", Z = 250'0.0" so that it moves up and behind the telephone pole. Select that last key frame in the time bar, hold down the
Shift key, and drag to frame 70. This should have created a copy of the
last key frame at frame 70.

This will make the droid pause for 10 frames.

The droid is behind the pole.

5   With the Animate button still on, drag the slider to frame 100 and move the droid to X = −130'0.0", Y = 1200'0.0", Z = 75'0.0" back behind the dumpster. Drag the slider to frame 120 and move the droid to X = −5'00.0", Y = 162'0.0", Z = 35'0.0".

Notice that it is above the puddle, but the puddle does not reflect it. In the next section, you will learn how to add the finishing scene effects.

There is no reflection of the droid in the puddle.

Making the Puddles Reflect the Droid

To add the last bit of reality to the scene, you want to make a reflection in the rain puddles when the droid flies over. To do this, you are going to create another Matte/Shadow material with a raytraced mask on it. This will enable the droid to reflect in the puddles only.

1   Open the Material Editor and select an empty sphere. Click the Standard button and select Matte/Shadow when the Material/Map Browser pops up.

2   Under the Matte/Shadow properties, make sure that both Opaque Alpha and Receive Shadows are checked. Set the Shadow Brightness to **1.0**. Under Reflection, click the Map button and select Mask. The Replace Map dialog will appear. Select Keep Old Map as Sub-map and click OK.

3   Click the Map button (it will say Map # bitmap). Under Bitmap Parameters, click the None button next to bitmap. Navigate to the Chapter 10 folder on the accompanying CD and select background.avi. This will give you a masking layer for the reflection. Click the None button next to the Mask, select Raytrace, and leave all the parameters as default.

4   Select the Ground plane and apply to it the material you just made. If you hit Render now, you should be able to see the reflection of the droid just barely. Remember that this is a dark scene, so that's why the reflection is not popping out. The next section will show you how to really help the visibility of the reflection and the droid!

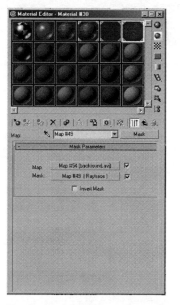

The mask material properties should look like this.

The Finishing Touches

You might have noticed that it is still difficult to see the droid reflected in the puddles. To put the final touches on this scene, you are going to add a simple glow in video post to the droid's antennas. This not only will make the droid show up better in the puddles, but will also illuminate it in the dark alley better. And, of course, all probe droids have lights on their antennae anyway, right?

1   Press "M" to open the Material Editor. Select the Red metal-looking sphere. To save time, this has already been applied to the top parts of the droid's antennae. Click the Material Effects Channel and set it to **1**.

2   Close the material and, in the top menu bar, select Rendering/Video Post. Click the little render teapot with the arrow to Add a Scene event. Camera 1 should already be highlighted; click OK at the bottom.

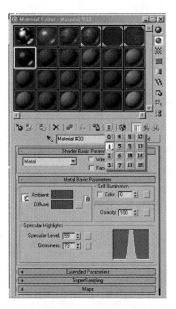

Set the Material Effects Channel to 1.

3   Click the yellow box with the wavy line that pops up to add an Image Filter event. Select Lens Effects Glow from the drop-down menu and select OK.

Select Lens Effect Glow from the drop-down list.

4   Click the yellow box with the down arrow. This will open the Add Image Output Event. Click Files and navigate to somewhere on your hard drive where you want to save the render. Select the format. I recommend a QuickTime movie, but you can use whatever you like. Click Save and then OK on the Image Output Event.

Specify in what format and where you want to save your render.

5   Now you will set up the glow. Double-click the Lens Effects Glow and click Setup in the pop-up box. This will bring up the Lens Effects Glow setup box. Before you do anything here, make sure your animation time slider is set to frame 105 so that the droid is in view and over a puddle. Click VP Queue and then click Preview. This will render the scene in the window.

6   Under the Properties tab/Source, deselect Object ID and select Effects ID. It is already set to **1**, which is what you set the Red Metal material to in the Material/Map Browser. You should see the scene rerender, but nothing looks different. Click the Preferences tab and set Effect/Size to **1.2.** Under Color, select User and set the Intensity to **60.0**.

7   After the scene rerenders, you should see a nice glow on the droid's antennas and in the puddle reflection. Click OK and you are ready to render the scene. Click the little running man at the top of the screen. In the Execute Video Post pop-up, select Range 0 to 120 and select your size under Output Size. Click Render and watch it go! (This is a perfect time for one of those Render Wonders that all of us computer animators are so familiar with.)

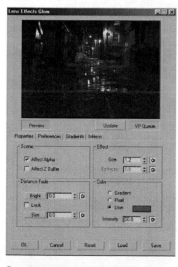

Set these parameters to achieve the proper glow.

Select your Output Size and render that sucker!

Note: For this first render, I recommend 320×240 so you can get a feel for what the scene looks like. When using your own models (or if you want to put this scene to tape), render 720×4865 for NTSC video. If you are sending it to a DV Tape, render at 720×480.

Note: To animate the arms, all you need to do is select a bone and move it up or down with the Animate button on. You can do that yourself if you want to. You can also make the droid rotate upside down and do all sorts of things. Be creative!

Modifications

Using your own models is the best way to customize this scene. You could add some more realism to this scene by adding spotlights to the droid. You might also want to try to create a particle system that acts like rain and bounces off the droid.

In this chapter's folder on the accompanying CD are a few other examples of other camera matching scenes I have done with still pictures. They are called Ship.avi and Swamp.avi. Have a look—maybe they will spark some ideas!

A character I created walking through a flat picture.

A spaceship landing in a flat picture of a swamp.

INDEX